THE WHITE MOUNTAIN GUIDE BOOK.

Samuel Coffin Eastman

CONCORD:
EDSON C. EASTMAN.
1858.

PREFACE.

It is hoped that this Guide will form the most complete, accurate and reliable Guide, yet published, to the Mountain Region of New Hampshire. Those before issued, have been rather guides *to* than *through* the Mountains, containing plentiful descriptions of places on the way, but scanty accounts of views and interesting scenes, really the object of the visit. Omissions and mistakes may, of course, occur. The editor is very solicitous to be favored with corrections of these, founded upon personal knowledge. Travellers willing to make such communications are requested to address them to the editor of the Guide Book, care of the Publisher.

The editor has been greatly assisted in the preparation of this book by Rev. THOMAS STARR KING of Boston, Mr. DANIEL GOODWIN, and Rev. AUGUSTUS WOODBURY of Providence, who have each contributed largely to its pages.

CONCORD, N. H., May 25th, 1858.

GUIDE.

NEW YORK TO WHITE MOUNTAINS.

From the city of New York, the point of immediate departure for Southern, Western, and we may add, a large portion of European travel into New England, seven distinct routes, more or less direct, lead to the White Mountain region of New Hampshire. Four of these, are laid through the city of Boston; one through the City of Worcester, Mass., and thence up the valley of the Merrimac River; one through the cities of New Haven, Hartford, and Springfield, up the valley of the Connecticut River, by railroad to Littleton, within three hours ride by stage-coach to Franconia; and the seventh by way of the Hudson River, by rail or boat, to Albany, thence to Rutland, and Bellows Falls, Vt., intersecting at the latter place with the route up the Connecticut.

The general view is as follows:

1. New York to Boston, via Stonington and Providence, on Long Island Sound by Steamboat to Stonington; thence to Providence and Boston by rail, arriving at Boston at 5 o'clock, A. M.

2. New York to Boston, via Newport and Fall River, on Long Island Sound by Steamboat; from Fall River by rail, arriving at Boston in season for the morning trains, North and East.

3. New York to Boston, via New London and Norwich, on Long Island Sound, by Steamboat to Allyn's Point; thence by rail through Worcester, arriving at Boston, about 5½, A.M.

4. New York to Boston, by railroad, via New Haven, Hartford, Springfield and Worcester. The cars leave New York, morning and afternoon, arriving at Boston about 4, P. M., and midnight.

On reaching Boston, the tourist has his choice of the three following routes:

(1.) Boston to Portland, over the Boston & Maine Railroad from Haymarket Square, passing through Andover and Lawrence, Mass., Exeter and Dover, N. H.; or the Eastern Railroad from Causeway Street, passing through Lynn, Salem and Newburyport, Mass., and Portsmouth, N. H. The two roads unite at South Berwick, Me. A third route is by the steamboats which leave the wharf at the foot of Milk street, every evening and arrive at Portland early in the morning. Arriving at Portland, in five hours from Boston, the traveller can immediately leave, (after refreshment,) for the "Alpine," or "Glen" House, Gorham, N. H., by the St. Lawrence & Atlantic Railroad, thus reaching the Eastern side of the Mountains the same day. The time by this route, is from New York to Boston, eleven hours; Boston to Portland, five hours; Portland to Gorham, four to five hours, or including detentions, not far from twenty-four hours. By taking one of the Sound boats in the afternoon, Gorham can be reached on the afternoon of the next day, without hurry or unusual fatigue.

(2.) Boston to Dover, N. H., by Boston & Maine Railroad; thence by Cocheco Railroad to Alton, N. H., at the southern end of Lake Winnipesaukee; thence by Steamer Dover, over the Lake to Wolfborough and Senter Harbor, dining on board the boat, and reaching Senter Harbor in season for a Stage Coach to Conway; thence to the Mountains by stage the next morning.

(3.) BOSTON TO CONCORD, N. H., by Boston & Maine, and Concord, Manchester & Lawrence Railroads, Haymarket Square, passing through Lawrence, Mass., and Manchester, N. H. At the latter place, a train from Boston, via Lowell and Nashua, over Lowell, (Causeway st.,) and Lowell & Nashua Railroads, unites with this route, and both streams of travel pour on together to Concord, N. H. Here connections are made with (*a*) the Northern Railroad, which connects at White River Junction with the route up the Connecticut. Passengers by this route reach Franconia, by way of Littleton, the same evening, at 9 o'clock. (*b*) The Montreal Railroad, by which passengers proceed to the Weirs' Station, Lake Winnipesaukee, whence the Steamer LADY OF THE LAKE, conveys them to Senter Harbor, in season for the afternoon stage to Conway. If the tourist desires to reach Franconia on the same day he passes by rail upon the same road, to Plymouth, N. H., where he stops to dine, at BURNHAM'S famous PEMIGEWASSET HOUSE, and takes the afternoon stage for the FLUME and PROFILE HOUSES, arriving at the latter about 9 o'clock, P. M., or he may go on to Littleton and arrive at the same time as by the Northern Railroad. Leaving New York, in the afternoon, one could reach Franconia or Conway, if he so desired, on the evening of the next day.

5. NEW YORK TO CONCORD, N. H., by way of Norwich, Worcester, and Nashua. The traveller reaches Worcester by rail, through New-Haven, &c., or by boat and rail, through Norwich. Connections are made directly with the Worcester & Nashua Railroad, and he proceeds without detention, except for refreshment, to Nashua, N. H. Here he takes the cars of the Concord Railroad for Concord, N. H., and has the choice of the routes enumerated above. The time required is the same as that for the preceding route.

6. NEW YORK TO FRANCONIA by rail except the last twelve miles from Littleton. The traveller by this route leaves New

York by the New-York & New-Haven Railroad, and proceeds as far as Springfield, Mass., without change of cars. At this place he takes the cars of the Connecticut River Railroad, passing through Northampton and Holyoke, and in sight of Mt. Tom on the west side, and Mt. Holyoke on the east side of the river, through Greenfield to South Vernon, Vt. From this place, the Vermont Valley Railroad passes through Brattleborough to Bellows Falls. Thence the route proceeds by Sullivan Railroad to Windsor, Vt.; thence by Vermont Central Railroad to White River Junction, where the route by Northern Railroad connects; thence by Passumpsic Railroad to Wells River; thence by White Mountains Railroad to Littleton, and thence by stage to Franconia. This route, after leaving Hartford, continues up the valley of the Connecticut, till it reaches Wells River, and affords a view of the beautiful scenery, which makes this valley a "garden of delight." The time is longer than by the other routes, as it requires two days to reach Franconia, but no one will regret the prolongation of the pleasant journey.

7. New York to Franconia, via Albany, Rutland, and Bellows Falls, Vt. Passengers leave New-York by Hudson River Railroad, or by boat, reaching Troy in season for the cars over the Rutland and Washington, or Western Vermont Railroad to Rutland, where they remain over night; leaving by early train the next morning, they reach Bellows Falls, in time to connect with the trains north, to Windsor, White River and Littleton, thus uniting at Bellows Falls, with the route just named. The time is the same as by route No. 6. This is without doubt the most beautiful and satisfactory of all the routes proposed. Besides the magnificently varied scenery of the Hudson, one enjoys to the highest degree the ride through the mountain State of Vermont. Her hills are covered with verdure to the very summits, and the little hamlets that nestle in

the valleys, are the abodes of comfort and happiness and virtue. There is, too,

"A newer life in every gale,"

as the fresh mountain air, with its invigorating influence, brings the roses to the cheeks, and vivifies the frame.

THE MOUNTAIN REGION.

After having given this preliminary view of the different approaches to the White Mountains, we propose to give a particular view of the Mountain region. After this is completed, we will give a more detailed account of the different routes before mentioned. We shall thus be enabled to give a greater symmetry to the whole book than could be obtained by first giving the routes *to*, and then *through* the region to be visited. As the various roads approach the mountains at different points we shall also avoid much needless repetition. The size of the book will thus be diminished while its convenience for consultation will be greatly increased.

We will commence, then, at Gorham, N. H., on the eastern side of the Mountains.

Gorham, N. H., is a thriving village which has been built up on the banks of the Androscoggin by the business which the Railroad and the Hotel have brought. The Alpine House, is one of the largest of the Hotels in the White Mountain region. It is the most substantially built of all. Under the charge of Mr. Hitchcock it is admirably kept. Passengers are deposited from the cars directly in front of the House as in the annexed picture. The main building is one hundred

View of Alpine House, Gorham, N. H.

feet in front by fifty in width, and is three stories high. There is an L of the same dimensions. The dining room is a noble hall eighty feet by thirty. The House can accommodate between two and three hundred guests.

The Alpine House is situated in a valley at the junction of the Androscoggin and Peabody rivers. The valley is 800 feet above the sea. The breadth of it is so great that the air is more dry, pure and bracing, than in the more narrow passes, directly under the lofty summits, where many of the larger public houses are placed. On this account, it has often been found more grateful and propitious to invalids, who are advised to try the mountain atmosphere. There is a post office in the Hotel. Mails are received every day from Montreal, and twice a day by railroad from Boston and Portland. To the other advantages must also be added a telegraph station connected with the Alpine House. Communication is thus practicable, at all times, with all parts of the United States and with Canada.

The scenery immediately around the Alpine House in the Gorham village, when the proper points are sought for enjoying it, is very interesting. It is the only spot from which the beauty of the range of Moriah, Carter, and the Imp can be seen to advantage. Mt. Carter is about 5,000 feet in height. The base from which it rises being much lower than the level of the Franconia Notch, the summit of Carter is really higher, as seen from Gorham, than Mt. Lafayette, the highest of the Franconia range, is from the lovely Echo Lake, near the Profile House. And there are few more charming spectacles among the mountains than the heavy shadows that are tangled in the deep-cut stairways of Mt. Carter, contrasted with the soft lights that lie on its steep, unbroken forests, in a clear summer afternoon. Mt. Moriah is some 200 feet lower than Mt. Carter, and is remarkable for the rolling, billowy lines that flow from its dome along its huge mass to the valley. It is, perhaps, the most graceful in its outline of any of the larger New Hampshire hills. The true position from which to detect its beauty and appreciate

View of Imp and Carter Mountains from Gorham.

its height, is at the bend of the Androscoggin, near "Lary's," about a mile above the Alpine House. If the visiter will take this walk just before a clear sunset, he will see the whole ridge bathed in the richest purple — a sight that is one of the richest rewards of a mountain journey. We regret that we have no sketch of Mt. Moriah. We give however a view of a portion of the range as seen from Gorham.

The lower mountain that stands between Moriah and Carter is called the Imp. This name has been given to it from the marked resemblance which the summit, seen from a certain point, bears to a grotesque human countenance. We give a drawing of the queer expression which the peak offers.

To get this view one must cross the Peabody river to the westerly side, in the afternoon. Leave the road to the Glen about two miles from the Glen House. Such a visit is a pleasant accompaniment to a ride from the Alpine House to the Glen; or it can be made directly from the Glen House, by those who are making their chief visit at that delightful spot.

The noble chain of hills to the north-west of the Alpine House is known as the Pilot range. The lines they cut against a clear and burning evening sky are very charming. To the east and south-east, Gorham is walled in by the stalwart and brawny Androscoggin hills. The noblest of these is Mt. Hayes directly behind the Alpine House. Its name was given in honor of Mrs. Hayes who was once associated as landlady in the management of the Hotel, and who is gratefully remembered by all guests who became acquainted with her. The mountain stands now the noblest external monument to her memory.

The first thing which travellers usually wish to know when they arrive in Gorham, is the distance to Mt. Washington, and the time and methods of making the ascent. Mt. Washington is eight miles distant from the Railroad Station in Gorham. Stages are in waiting at every train to convey passengers to the Glen House, which is situated directly at its base. The ascent of the mountain, however, may be made from either house. If travellers are in a hurry to reach the Glen House, and prefer to start from that point, they ride in the stages eight miles to that hotel, and take horses there. The landlord of the Alpine House also keeps a stable of excellent mountain ponies near the foot of Mt. Washington. If travellers desire, therefore, they can have a wagon from Gorham, be driven to the base of the mountain, take ponies and guide there, make the ascent, and stay at the Glen House when they descend, or ride back at once to the Alpine House. The road is precisely the same, and the expense the same, in whichever way the excursion is made. It is well to know, however, that horses and guides are furnished from Gorham as well as from the Glen. For it sometimes happens that travellers arrive in Gorham by the eleven o'clock forenoon train from Portland, who would like to make the ascent of Mt. Washington that day, and return to Portland, or go on to Montreal, the next morning. This is almost always practicable, and has often been done from Gorham. By taking a wagon from the Alpine House, the base of Mt. Washington is reached quicker than by stage; the ascent is made in the afternoon; and the conveyance is in waiting to return the passenger, as soon as he descends, to the Alpine House again.

But if travellers are not in a great hurry, they should certainly make their plans to see the striking scenery that is offered near the Alpine House. No point in the whole mountain region presents more attractions within reach of a short and delightful wagon drive, a pleasant horseback-ride up a bridle path, or a tolerably easy mountain-scramble. The first of these excursions to which we will call attention is that to

The Lead Mine Bridge.

The name is derived from an abandoned lead-mine about six miles below Gorham, on the eastern bank of the Androscoggin, in Shelburne. The Bridge is about four miles from the Alpine House. The proper time to visit it is in the latter part of a summer afternoon, when the golden light is on the meadows, and the long shadows are falling athwart the mountains. There is no spot in the whole mountain region where the beauty of a river is joined so charmingly to the majesty of the hills. No river-view can be more fascinating than that of the noble Androscoggin breaking around emerald islands with clean sandy shores, and joining its parted currents again into one strong tide just above the bridge where one stands. And then a few miles distant, enthroned over the narrow valley, as though the stream flowed directly from their base, rises the heavy dome of Mt. Washington, in company with the clear-cut exquisite pyramid of Madison.

The height of the noblest mountains is never appreciated by going close to their base, if they are foreshortened by ridges intervening between the eye and the supreme summits. The Lead-mine Bridge is just far enough away from the White hills to allow their height to make its true impression. And whoever sees Mt. Madison thus, in a clear afternoon, will recall the impression it makes, as perhaps the loveliest picture which the White Mountain journey leaves in the memory. Three hours from the Alpine House will give ample time for the excursion. Teams and drivers are always in readiness for the accommodation of guests.

Next among the privileges of Gorham we must speak of a drive from the Alpine House to

Randolph Hill.

This hill is on the road to the villages of Randolph and Jefferson, and is about five miles from the hotel. There is no climbing to be done; the wagon is driven directly to the summit, and the road is excellent. By this drive one is taken directly to the northerly base of Madison and Jefferson. He sees the whole northerly wall of the Mt. Washington range from crest to valley. The height is far greater than the wall of the Crawford Notch. There is no point, where standing so near, any of the White Mountains look so lofty and so grand. Certainly no valley view can be gained of Mt. Washington that compares with the grandeur of Jefferson from this position. Only a suggestion of the sublimity of this view is given in the plate which we introduce. The sense of height, the tremendous mass, the grand masonry, the rich forest-verdure, the silence, the twin outlines of the two mountains, and the symmetry of the grey and blasted peaks that rise and face each other above the vast wilderness that clothes their sides, combine to make an impression on the eye and soul that years will not efface. A traveller should not fail to take this view, if possible; and no discomfort is connected with the excursion. An hour is sufficient for the drive to Randolph Hill from the Alpine House; and three quarters of an hour for the return.

We must call attention, next, to

Berlin Falls.

Those who love water-views and cataract-scenery will say that these Falls are the richest of all the attractions that invest Gorham. They are situated six miles from the Alpine House. But the road that leads to them is excellent; the drive is taken

View of Mts. Madison and Jefferson from Randolph Hill.

in an hour; and the scenery on the way, along the banks of the Androscoggin, is continually noble, wild, and stimulating. It is no rivulet or mountain cascade one visits at Berlin. The whole Androscoggin, fed from a branch of Lake Umbagog, and never low even in a drought, like the Upper Connecticut, pours here down a rocky gateway. It is a long swift rapid, broken here and there by a direct and powerful fall. In the course of two miles the river descends more than two hundred feet. The road winds directly by the river, and there is no hard clambering or wet walking in the excursion.

View of Berlin Falls.

The first view as one alights from the wagon reveals the river for a quarter of a mile flecked with little white caps at the uppermost rapids, then plunging in a winding rush of foam, then calmed again, and flowing with its ruffled caps towards Gorham. After taking this general look, which is very fascinating, we must select points for observing the heavier pitches of the river, and estimating the force of the cataract. We must go down upon a jutting rock that faces the sweeping tide, and see the last leap of the mad tide over a huge boulder, before it settles into common rapids again; we must go up and stand on the bridge that crosses the narrowest gully, and watch the foam sweep underneath like a race-horse—the backwater from each side overlaying the central current, so that it rushes in wedge shape, or like an enormous flatiron, nose first, through the gorge; especially must we go last above the bridge, and sit down upon the rocks, to watch, at leisure, the first and deepest plunge of the river. Although the bridge is very near, one has no conception, in looking from it, of the grandeur of this portion of the fall. One can sit by it for an hour with increasing delight. Visitors have said that it repaid for the cost and time of a visit to the mountains, and that all the other scenery was extra. The power of this part of the fall is so satisfactory, the quantity of water so great, and the flood of foam that sweeps away from it so full of life, that we have never been able to recall, while sitting there, aught that surpasses it in the suggestion of power, but the English fall at Niagara. We quote the declaration of a prominent poet of New England, given with emphasis on the spot once, in our hearing, when we say that it is better worth visiting than the falls of St. Anthony.

There should be a small and well-kept public house at Berlin, that visitors might have leisure, and the cool parts of the day, and especially a full-moonlight evening, for wandering around the banks, and enjoying the rapids and plunges of the river.

A visit to the falls is easily made from the Alpine House between breakfast and dinner, or in the afternoon before tea. But one needs to go several times, as at Trenton, and also to have leisure for studying the grand forms and summits of the outer White Mountains, which tower with a symmetry that does not disturb their solid and serious majesty, a little to the west. In fact, the mountain panorama, visible from the road just above the falls, is one of the most inspiring to be found within the compass of the New Hampshire tour. But noontime is the worst season for a visit to the cataract, on account of heat. In July or August, a cool day, or a cloudy one, would be best.

It would be among the richest joys of a September visit to Gorham, to give the heart of one of its clear bracing days to an excursion along the Androscoggin—dining on the rocks above the bridge; and, returning towards sunset, to face for the most of the way, the great White Mountain range, stained with a glorious brown light, and the range of Moriah and Carter, lifting purple peaks and ridges against the blue southern sky.

But besides the attractions to be reached by wagon rides, there are excursions to be made from the Alpine House, on horseback or on foot, that must be spoken of.

THE ASCENT OF MT. MORIAH

is the first to be named. There is an excellent bridle-path to the summit, and a large log cabin has been built there, for partial protection against a squall or a thunder shower that might overtake a party on the ridge. The mountain is just 4,700 feet in height. Most of the way the path is cut through the fresh, rich wilderness.

What can be more delightful than a ride on a clever horse up such a mountain path? The air is so fresh and fragrant! The sun chequers the mosses, and the pale, undecayed leaves of the previous Autumn so charmingly with spots of light, that shifts as the wind plays with the overhanging leaves! The crackling of branches under the horse's hoofs has a cheery sound. Old rocks, soft with moss, and dripping with moisture, tell you that you are invading a sanctuary that had been sacred for centuries from the foot of man.

Now and then, through the trees, a glimpse is gained of a grand coliseum of pines on the steep and crescent sides of a near mountain, from which a ravine separates you. Now and then, you come upon some bare ledge or shoulder, from which you look down the valley of the Androscoggin for miles, and admire the forethought of nature in leaving this easy track among these billowy ridges of land, for the Atlantic & St. Lawrence road. Soon you plunge into the woods again, and are borne up and up by the panting horse till the shrubs begin to grow scanty, and suddenly you are on the desolate and jagged peak. What a view! The face of nature seems to have been torn by some mighty harrow. The eye must travel far to the southwest to rest upon any extent of level land. Northern New Hampshire, Vermont and Maine, is a vast panorama of solid surges. On the west, the distant view is barred by the heavy forms of the great White Mountain range proper.

In this respect a visit to Mt. Moriah is more interesting than to Mt. Washington; for here Mt. Washington is part of the landscape. Its height and mass, and the grandeur of its fellow peaks, can be relatively measured, as they cannot when one stands on their ridges. The whole excursion can easily be made in five hours;—two hours to ascend, a little less to return, and about an hour on the summit.

But it may be that the traveller does not care to make an ascent of a mountain so high as this, in addition to the ascent of Mt. Washington, or instead of that ascent. We will call attention, therefore, to

Mount Surprise,

and the charm of the prospect that is opened from it. This mountain is directly in front of the Alpine House. It is in fact one of the spurs of Mt. Moriah, and is about 1,200 feet in height. The bridle-path to the top is not difficult at all in the ascent. Good walkers can gain the crest without trouble in an hour, and can return in half that time. It is an easy and charming horseback excursion for ladies. And the view which the summit offers is different in character from any that we recall in the mountain region. It suggests the marvellous picture of the Notch seen from Mt. Willard. The height of Mt. Surprise is about the same as that of Mt. Willard. And it commands the great cleft between Mt. Carter and the White Mountains, through which the Peabody river flows, as Mt. Willard commands the Notch and the infant Saco.

The top of Mt. Surprise is worth visiting, apart from the view it furnishes, for the savage revelation it offers of the ruin which fire and winds can work on the hills. Scores of great tree-trunks, stripped, charred and half-consumed, are heaped and twisted over an acre or two of the crest and side of the hill, in impressive confusion. The whole scene is the hieroglyphic autobiography, it may be, of the destructive partnership of July lightning and January gale. The chief payment for the ascent, however, is not this broad "charcoal sketch" of ravage, but the sight, gained amid that dingy desolation, of the grandest portions of the White Mountain ridge. The highest summits of the range rise directly against the eye. There is no intervening ridge, or obstacle. You look down 1,200 feet to the bed of the Peabody which is fed from the great range, and up along the unbroken forests to the peak of Mt. Madison, the crest of Jefferson that overtops it, and at the southwest of these, the summit of Adams, and the mass of Mt. Washington. There is no other eminence where one can get so near to these monarchs, and receive such an impression of their sublimity, the vigor of their outlines, their awful solitude, and the extent of the wilderness which they bear up on their slopes. The scene is so wild and glorious, and the cost of labor to gain it so slight, that it is a pity any visitants of the eastern side of the mountains should fail to add it to their treasures of memory. And besides this view of the great range, the outlook from Mt. Surprise over the mountains of the North, and up the valley through which the Androscoggin twists its way, is very grand. On horseback from the Alpine House, the whole jaunt can be made in two hours and a half, with ample time for the Summit.

We have already spoken of

MOUNT HAYES,

which rises just behind the Alpine House, beyond the Androscoggin. If there were a bridle-path to the top of this eminence, it would soon be celebrated as affording the grandest landscape view of Madison, Jefferson, and Washington to be obtained in New Hampshire. As it is, every man who visits Gorham and who has a love of mountain scrambles, may well be urged to obtain the services of Mr. Gordon, as guide, and scale Mt. Hayes. About two hours from the base will be sufficient to gain the top. The picture from the summit cannot be sufficiently praised. The view of Jefferson, and Madison, sweeping from the uplands of Randolph will never be forgotten. And Mt. Washington shows no such height, or grandeur, when seen from any other point. Mt. Washington does not show its superior height, or look grander in form than the associated peaks, from any position in the *valleys* near Gorham and the Glen. But from Mt. Hayes its supereminence and majesty are caught and appreciated. That summit seems to be the chair set by Providence at the right distance and angle to observe and enjoy its majesty, its symmetry, and the proud grace with which its "airy citadel" is sustained against the sky. And by way of *dessert* to this substantial feast of mountain grandeur, a most charming view of the curves of the Androscoggin for twenty miles, of its exquisite islands, and of the meadows which it threads, is given from Mt. Hayes.

There is another pedestrian excursion possible from Gorham, of which we should not fail to speak. We mean, the

Ascent of Mt. Madison,

from the foot of Randolph Hill, and a visit to the northerly ridge and summits of the White Mountain group. To those who love mountain climbing and the wildest scenery which the hills can exhibit, no more tempting expedition than this can be proposed. Several parties made this excursion last year, sometimes camping out in a ravine, or on the ridge. Their reports of the grandeur and magnificence of the views that rewarded their toil are very inspiring. A company of strong pedestrians, starting from the Alpine House, Gorham, early in the morning, and riding to the base of Mt. Madison, at the foot of Randolph

Hill, could ascend Mt. Madison, pass over its summit, around or over the sharp pyramid of Jefferson, over Adams, between the humps of Mt. Clay, and reach the house on the top of Mt. Washington, before sunset.

Such a route would lie among and over the largest mountains of the range. Between Madison and Jefferson, the party would see the noblest outlines of rocky precipice and crest which the whole range can furnish; for they would stand directly between the steep pinnacles of those noble hills, that spring from the ridge. They could climb to the sharp apex of Jefferson. They would see the glorious picture of Washington that starts out in crossing from Jefferson to Adams. The long easterly slope is shown from its base in the Pinkham forests; the cone towers sheer out of "The Gulf of Mexico;" and every rod of the bridle-path is visible from the Ledge to the Summit House.

And the route brings into view all the great ravines of the range, except "Tuckerman's." One will see the long and narrow gully between Madison and Jefferson, and the tremendous hollow of Jefferson itself on the north, which was climbed for the first time in 1857, by a party formed by the writer, and which is now called by the guides, "King's Ravine." He will see the precipitous gulf between Jefferson and Adams on the southeast; the deep cut gorge in Adams, on the northwest, whose bones of grey cliff, breaking bare through the steep verdure, will be remembered as the most picturesque of all the scenes which the day gives. He will wind around the chasm between Adams and Clay, divided from the savage "Gulf of Mexico" by a spur of Adams, that runs out toward the Glen House. And he will gaze off with delight upon the long rolling braces that prop Mt. Pleasant, and Franklin, and the tawny Monroe,—the boundaries of the ravines that one sees in riding to Mt. Washington from the Notch, over the Crawford bridle-path.

A path through the forest of Mt. Madison to the summit, from the foot of Randolph Hill, has been "blazed," by Mr.

Gordon, of Gorham. No more competent or faithful guide than Mr. Gordon, could be desired for this expedition, or for the ascent of Mt. Hayes, or for any tramp among the unvisited portions of the mountains. He has, several times, accompanied exploring and visiting parties to Umbagog Lake, which can be reached in about a day from Gorham. Travellers can easily learn at the Alpine House how to engage him for any service.

Before turning from the scenery around Gorham, we must speak of the stage routes from Gorham to "The Notch." There are two roads, One passes through the Glen, the Pinkham forest, the village of Jackson, and up through Bartlett to the Crawford House, which is just beyond the Notch itself. The distance from Gorham by this route, is forty-four miles; from "The Glen," thirty-six miles. The stages do not start from Gorham, but from the Glen House. They leave about 8 o'clock in the morning. Travellers, therefore, who desire to go by this road must be at the Glen House over night, or must take a ride of eight miles from the Alpine House to the Glen, early in the morning, in order to reach the stage.

There is another route from Gorham to the Notch, by what is called "THE CHERRY MOUNTAIN ROAD." The distance by this route is thirty-two miles. There are no regular stages over it, as over the road from the Glen House. But Mr. Hitchcock, the landlord of the Alpine House, provides excellent teams and drivers for all parties who wish to reach the Notch by this road. The price of seats in these extra teams, is, we believe, but little more than the regular stage fares amount to, from Gorham, by the other route.

It is to be regretted that there is not a regular line of stages by this route to the Notch. For the scenery along almost the whole line of the road is grander than by any other stage route among the mountains. It takes in the glorious spectacle from Randolph Hill, of which we have spoken. It commands every slope and summit of the Mt. Washington range from the north; and for some twelve miles of the way they are all in view at once, with no intervening hills to break the impression of their majesty. Such a view can be gained on no other road; and the forms of the mountains on the northerly slope are grander than on the southerly side. From the village of Jefferson, through which this Cherry Mountain road runs, not only is every one of the great White Mountain group visible, but also the Franconia Mountains, the side of the Willey Mountain in the Notch, the line of nearer Green Mountains beyond the Connecticut,—in fact, a panorama of hills to the northwest and north, almost as fine as the prospect in that direction from the summit of Mt. Washington. So striking is the view from the village of Jefferson that, doubtless, if a good hotel should be built there, that village would be one of the most popular resorts in New England before many years. To see this picture would richly repay a drive from Gorham and return, if the traveller did not desire to pass on to the Notch. The noblest part of the view can be had without leaving the wagon, from a hill in Jefferson, about twelve miles from the Alpine House.

The return ride from the Notch to Gorham, by Cherry Mountain, is, in some respects, superior to the ride the other way. From Jefferson to Gorham, it is certainly more grand, than when facing in the other direction.

For several miles we front the four highest mountains of the ridge, and seem to be riding into them, with no chance of a detour. How massive they seem as we draw nearer and nearer! The summits appear of about equal height, and instead of presenting thin and gullied sides, all their lines run outward towards us and are firmly braced in the valley, as though they were immense forts, once upheaved and buttressed with granite ridges, to defend an army of a larger mould than our race, against a siege. The Notch itself is hardly more majestic than this quadruple fortification, which glooms and darkens more and more upon the eye as we ride nearer to it, and which springs out of a wild forest as yet almost unvisited by man. For several miles the vision lasts. Then Washington drops away from the company, and we are left with Adams, Jefferson, and Madison. Next, Adams withdraws, and we ride by the base of the remaining two. Soon their grand lines untwist, and their rocks seem, as it were, to be dishevelled, till we gain the summit of Randolph Hill, overlooking Gorham, and find that, by inexplicable magic they have been transformed into superb symmetry again, and hide from the delighted eye every trace of those glorious compeers, that had joined with them in threatening the valley of Randolph, a few miles behind.

Parties may feel reasonably sure that they can obtain excellent wagons and experienced drivers for this Cherry Mountain route, at any time, from Mr. Hitchcock of the Alpine House in Gorham. And so many parties are sent in this way to the Notch, that travellers staying at the Crawford House can very often find, on inquiry, teams about to return to Gorham, that will enable them to view the magnificent scenery of the return ride.

The proprietor of the Alpine House is also prepared to furnish carriages and drivers to parties of any size for a tour of the mountains, as well as for a visit to the Notch.

And now let us turn to

The Glen.

This charming spot is situated eight miles, as we have said, from Gorham. Until the opening of the Atlantic & St. Lawrence Railroad, a few years ago, it was an unvisited waste. At first a Public House of very modest proportion was erected. Soon it was found necessary to enlarge it, and then to increase its size again; and now one of the largest and grandest Hotels of the White Mountain region stands there for the benefit of travellers. The main building is 130 feet in length, 42 in width, and four stories high. There is a grand portico to the principal entrance. Over this is a balcony upon which the second story windows open, from which may be had an uninterrupted view of the five highest mountains of New England.

From this balcony, also, the guests of the Hotel can watch with a glass the progress of the horseback parties ascending or descending the rugged ledges of Mt. Washington. The dining room is a noble hall calculated to seat two hundred persons; and the withdrawing rooms, which front towards the Mountains and the rushing Peabody river, are spacious, airy, and exceedingly pleasant.

The Glen House, since the commencement, has been under the charge of Mr. J. M. Thompson. How acceptably he has fulfilled his duty as proprietor and landlord is attested, better than any words of ours can describe, by the crowds that seek his hospitality, in the hottest weeks of summer, from all parts of the country. Spacious as the Hotel is, it often overflows with guests in August.

We give a picture of the Glen House. But the plate does no justice to its situation. It stands on a plateau, 830 feet above the Gorham valley, and 1,632 feet above tide water at Portland, in the midst of a magnificent mountain bowl. Behind it bend the thin high ridges of Mt. Carter and its spurs, 3,000 feet in height, and green with unbroken forests to their crests. On the southwest, one sees the steep, bony braces of Mt. Washington, running off one behind the other into the Pinkham forests and towards Jackson. Directly in front are the outworks and huge shoulder of Mt. Washington itself, and behind this heavy shoulder, on a retreating ridge, the pinnacle where the Summit House stands. Associated directly with Mt. Washington, and bending around to the north-west and north, are Mt. Clay, rising over the huge "Gulf of Mexico;" the stout, square shouldered Adams; and the symmetrical, sharp, and splendid pyramid of Jefferson, with its peak so pointed that it looks unscaleable. This mountain is by far the grandest in shape and impressiveness of all. And next to this with lines running eastward is Mt. Madison which completes the staff of Washington. Thus the five highest summits of the White Hills

View of the Glen House.

are, as we have said, in full view directly in front of the Hotel in the Glen. The height of Mt. Washington is 6,285 feet; Mt. Clay, 5,011; Mt. Adams, 5,710; Mt. Jefferson, 5,790; Mt. Madison, 5,361.

No Public House among the Mountains is situated so near the Mt. Washington range as this. There are views of the Mountains to be had at a little greater distance that will give more pleasure to the artistic sense; but no view of the chief White Mountain range can be had from a Hotel that is comparable with this which the piazza of ths Glen House offers.

The best time to approach it is in the clear afternoon of a summer day, when the shadows fall soft and rich in the gorges and over the rugged slopes of the chain. Then the mountains look higher, and their grandeur is tempered with a mystic beauty. There is perpetual charm, too, in watching the play of the vapors around the cliffs and in the ravines, on a misty and showery day in August. Now they will wrap a long mountain wall in a cold, grey mantle to the base. Now they will break along a ridge, and reveal the harsh sides of a chasm, or the ramparts of a ridge, hanging seemingly in the clouds. Soon they will thin away below for a mile, and show the green foreground softened by a moist veil. Next they will knot themselves into thick rolls, and then stretch themselves slowly into sleazy textures, as though they were made of vapory India rubber. Once in a while, they will lift themselves nearly to the summit of a ridge, and try to plunge down again,—really tiring the eye that watchs them

Sink by compulsion and laborious flight.

And sometimes they will break entirely around one of the mountains, Jefferson perhaps, and show it piercing the grey sky, apparently doubled in height by being seen isolated from its brother hills.

In May and early June the view from the Glen House is very charming. For then huge patches of snow lie on the upper slopes of the range. But in October the spectacle is generally more fascinating than in any other season of the year. Especially when the traveller can see, as we once saw there, the summits, stained with snow, rising over forests dyed in orange, brown, and crimson,—and delicate curtains of mist drooping from the sky and swaying gently along the line of the crests.

Stages leave the Glen House, every morning, for the Notch, by the way of Jackson, and for North Conway, and Conway. The distance to the Notch, as we have said, is thirty-six miles; to North Conway twenty miles; to Conway twenty-five miles. Stages run, also, to the Gorham and the Alpine house, connecting with four trains on the Atlantic & St. Lawrence Road. And from each train, up and down, on that road there is stage conveyance from Gorham to the Glen.

Of course the chief object of interest among the guests at the Glen House, after faithfully seeing the mountain view, is

The Ascent of Mt. Washington.

More travellers ascend Mt. Washington now from the Glen House and the Alpine House, by the road from the Glen, than by any other route. The distance from the base of the mountain, in front of the Glen House, to the summit is a little less than six miles. Four miles of this distance are passed on the easy slope of the road designed for a carriage route to the summit. The project of such a road was started some four years ago. It was supposed that the road would be completed last year (1857.) But the enterprise seems of late to be suspended. Part of the way, the path has been finished and macadamized. It winds upward with a very easy grade—one foot in eight—and inclines inward towards the mountain, so that the rains shall not wash heavily across it. And it is laid out with sufficient width to allow carriages to pass each other. The road, if finished according to the plan, would be eight miles in length.

Only a small portion of the track has been completed so that a carriage could be driven over it. But it has been laid out and partially built for about four miles; and over this distance, the parties who ascend from the Glen and Gorham ride on horseback up a very easy grade. The horses then reach the top of what is called "The Ledge." From this point the distance is but two miles to the summit of Mt. Washington; and along these two miles the glories, as well as the only difficulties, of the ascent are found.

The charm of the bridle-path from *the Notch* to Mt. Washington, lies in the passage over the tops of four lower summits of the ridge, each one a little higher than the last, and in the view thus given, of ravines that sweep off, each way, from the horse path to the base of the range. From *the Glen* the ascent is made directly up Mt. Washington itself all the way.

And during the last two miles a most surprising view is offered of Adams, Jefferson, and Madison. They sweep up from the enormous Gulfs at the right hand of the path, and are visible from base to crown.

There is no view, perhaps, so exciting as this, on the path we have just spoken of from the Crawford Notch. Many will think that this spectacle, which grows grander and grander as they rise, is more inspiring than the prospect from the peak above. One learns, in looking at those great forms, the decided difference there is in *genus* between a mountain and a hill. The eye is fascinated by the colors of these rugged monarchs—the various verdure of their lower forests, their tawny shoulders, the purple and grey of their bare ledges, the dim green of their peaks. One will notice, also, the charming lines which the torrents have torn upon their surfaces. For when we look across a gulf, or from a little distance below, upon a steep mountain, we find that it is the wrath of the freshets that gives them their finest lines of expression and character. And if the day is blessed with clouds that drift over the mountains, the eye will find unspeakable pleasure in watching the shadows that will droop swiftly from cone to base; and in following the incessant flushes and frolics of light and shade, that robe them with ever changing charm.

But to appreciate the beauty and majesty of these mountains that are in view from the Glen House and Gorham path, one should see them late on a bright summer afternoon, either in ascending or descending Mt. Washington. Then the sun is behind them, sinking in the west. Then the richest contrasts of color, of light, and of shadow are revealed. The summit an shoulders of Mt. Adams glow with rich orange hues. The slanting light streams between the peaks and burnishes the sides of their ragged pyramids. The "Gulf of Mexico" gapes with more terror as the shadows from its walls, that measure more than a thousand feet, fall far into its base. And as the sun falls nearer and nearer the horizon, the sharp shadows of Mt. Jefferson, and of the neighboring peaks, stream down upon the Glen House valley, and march up the opposite slopes of Carter to dislodge its yellow light that melts into purple, and to cover them with dusk. The noon-time is the poorest of all seasons to be on the ridge of Mt. Washington; for then there are no shadows. And it is a pity that the great majority of those who ascend the range, see the scenery during the most unpoetic hours, near midday.

From the summit of "The Ledge," where the view of the three great mountains we have been speaking of is first gained, the path rises over a series of receding plateaus. Each seems to be the summit, as one looks from below. It is on account of this structure of the cone of Mt. Washington, that it fails to show its real height, until one gets far enough off from it, in the valleys, to escape the effect of foreshortening.

During the last part of the ascent, one will see the pile of stones that marks the spot where Miss Bourne, of Kennebunk, Me., died, near midnight, in September, 1856, and where her uncle and cousin kept sad watch till dawn. They started in the afternoon, without a guide, to walk to the Summit. Night and fog overtook them; and the young lady perished in the chill and darkness among the rocks, but a few rods from the

3*

house they were in search of. Quite near, also, is the shelving rock, beneath which the remains of an elderly gentleman from Wilmington, Del., were found in July, 1857. He had attempted to ascend the mountain alone, one afternoon in August of the year before, and must have been overtaken by storm, and cold, and darkness, near the summit. His watch, and some Bank bills in his vest pocket, were found uninjured; though most of the body, and even part of the skeleton, were gone. A little further below, and at the left of the ascending path, the ledge is visible where Dr. Benjamin Ball, of Boston, passed two nights in the snow and sleet of an October storm, alone, without food or covering. He was rescued when nature was about sinking. His feet were frozen, and he could not speak. How his life was preserved in such exposure is a marvel. It is equally remarkable that, though his feet were severely frozen, they were saved.

Now let us ascend the last part of the steep cone and stand upon the summit. The time used in making the journey from the base in the Glen to the peak, is generally about three hours. It is often done in two hours and a half, and has been accomplished in less than two hours. What a stupendous view! A horizon of nearly six hundred miles! At first nothing is discerned but mountain sentinels on every hand, over furrowed valleys! We look on the rocky warts and bristly wrinkles of the hide of New England!

If the day is clear, one can see Monadnock loom as a pale blue film, a hundred miles off on the southwest. Far in the east, Katahdin is driven like a wedge into the sky. Westward the eye roams almost to the Catskills; northward into Canada, far beyond the sources of the Connecticut; southward, to the mouth of the Saco. In a clear morning, or evening, if there is a silvery gleam on the south-eastern horizon, it tells that the sun is shining on the sea off Portland.

Nearer to us, on the west, towers the gloomy ridge of Franconia, subsiding towards the Merrimack. That flash now and then, through the opaline southern air is from Winnipisaukee, the most exquisite jewel in the Lake-necklace of New England. On the near north, the twin-domed Stratford mountains tower. Their barren pallor, seen through the uncertain air, counterfeits snow. The cloven Pinkham pass lies directly beneath us, bending around to lovely North Conway. Over this last village we observe the drooping shoulders of Kearsarge, whose northern sides flow from the summit as softly as full folds of drapery fall from a ring. Mt. Crawford attracts attention by his singular knob-like crest; and near him, all the winding Bartlett hills stand up, guarding the shy beauty of their intervales. The long and solid "Pleasant Mountain" draws the eye, set so squarely near the still silver of Lovell's pond. And farther south, the dim, level, leopard-spotted land stretches wide to the horizon-haze.

Of course, it is unwise to attempt to describe such a view. It is the map of New England printed before us in glowing poetry. Those who look upon the sublime diorama for the first time, under favorable circumstances, are so oppressed by the novelty and grandeur, that they do not appreciate what they have seen till some days afterwards. Then it rises in memory, and becomes a perpetual treasure for "the mind's eye." No one should fail to make the ascent, if health is good. There is no danger worth calculating; and the fatigue that may be incurred is nothing to the spectacle that is offered. Especially are the temptations to ascend greater now to ladies and partial invalids, since such admirable accommodation is found in the little hotel on the Summit.

There have been, and are still, we believe, serious disputes about the title to the acre or two of chippy rock that make the crown of Mt. Washington. There have even been rival hotels on its apex, the "TIP TOP HOUSE," and the "SUMMIT HOUSE." Both these Houses have been united now under one management. They were kept in 1857 by Messrs. Hall & Spalding;

and everything that could be done on such a height, 6,300 feet above the sea, for the comfort of guests, was faithfully attended to by them.

When we think what a labor it is to carry all provisions to such an elevation, and that even fuel must be taken up from the forests far below, we cannot fail to admire the forethought and energy that have kept the Summit House so well. Good coffee and tea with milk, fresh eggs, new and well-made bread, generally fresh meats, as well as excellent ham, and often trout, are found on the plentifully provided table. Those who ascended Mt. Washington before there was any shelter on the peak from gale or shower, or driving scud, or snow-squall, that often awaited or overtook them, will know how those are favored now who find good protection, fire, and a hot dinner ready on the top. The charges are certainly not unreasonable,—a dollar for each meal, and a dollar for lodging. Sheets of paper and envelopes, each with an engraving of the Mountain house and Summit, are on sale there. Letters written thus to friends are mailed to all parts of the country by the proprietors of the hotel. They drop the summer out of their calendar, and make their home for days above human fellowship, amid lightning and thunder, blinding fogs and sweeping sleet, to offer such service to travellers.

It is frequently the case that persons pass up from the Glen to the Summit, and either walk or ride down on the other side to the Notch ; and vice versa. In this way a day's time, and a stage ride of over thirty miles is saved. A great many, too, remain over night on the summit. Unless the weather has long been stormy, or very damp, one can sleep in comfort and safety in the Summit House. A night there in which one can see a clear sunset, a moonrise, and a sunrise, is a privilege that we will not attempt to describe. One appreciates the height of Mt. Washington more by looking up in the night to the mighty dome of stars, than by looking off and below in the day. Or if the night is wild and stormy, the feeling one gains there of the tremendous forces amid which we are placed on this globe, will more than atone for any uneasiness or discomfort. We advise all who can, to remain over night on Mt. Washington.

But it is time to turn from the hospitality of the Summit House, and descend, through the exciting views that lie around Mt. Washington, to the Glen House once more, We have not spoken of other attractions that belong to its neighborhood. One of these is a ride to "THE IMP," which we described in connection with Gorham. The point, as we have already said, from which the face with its quaint expression upon the mountain top is seen, is nearly two miles from the Glen House, on the road that diverges from the road to the Alpine House, and which leads towards Randolph. It would be, also, a pleasant afternoon walk.

Let us attend next to

THE GLEN ELLIS FALL.

This cataract is one of the interesting features of the wild scenery in the neighborhood of the Glen House. Carriages run regularly from the hotel to carry visitors.

The fall is about four miles from the Glen House, near the road to North Conway and the Notch. It is very easy of access from the point where you leave the wagon. Five minutes walk through the forest takes one within hearing of the rich roar that announces the nearness of the cataract. A critical ear could construct the form and grandeur of the fall from its voice. Its bass quality, not broad and massive, but youthful, vigorous and intense, and the slight splashiness that boarders and thins its baritone, foretell that we are to come upon a narrow cataract, leaping from a great height, with concentrated stream, into a shallow basin. But the sound does not prepare a stranger for the startling view upon which the forest path suddenly opens. From the carriage road, the foot track is nearly level, leading to a tree that overhangs a precipice of more than a hundred feet. We lean against this tree for support, not without misgivings as to its roots, and look down upon a huge wall of rock, over which the Ellis river, stranding the streams of its various brooks into a huge liquid cable, whose constant friction has worn a deep groove in the granite, slides at a very sharp angle, for some twenty feet, and then leaps, as from the nose of a gigantic pitcher, sixty feet more. The public (as well as the cascade,)

View of Glen Ellis Fall.

are indebted to Mr. Shepley, of Portland, for changing its name from "Pitcher Fall," which was first given to it, to the more elegant and appropriate title "Glen Ellis Cataract."

To discover the most romantic and charming combinations in mountain scenery, one must explore the larger streams, on their way to the open valleys. The Naiads know how to turn their course through the most picturesque passes, under the richest arches of forest boughs, and down the most bewitching dells. This is one of the glorious perquisites of the devoted troutfisher, that his profession, (for it is really one of the fine arts) leads him along the bye-ways of beauty that are hidden from the eyes of ease-loving travellers, and up through winding cascade-aisles to many an adytum of forest wildness, or mountain grandeur. Probably some trout-fisher was the discoverer of Glen Ellis Fall, which has been known only a few years. The first sight of it must have given a most impressive joy to the explorer, if he were a man of taste.

The spot where it pours is more wild, and combines more of the elements of loneliness, untameableness, lawless beauty, and strong contrasts of features, than any other spot in the White Mountain region. The overhanging tree against which the visitor leans to look down at the water-fall, giving him a footing that undermines his delight with a sense of insecurity and fear; the steep, mountain wall opposite, more than three thousand feet high, and thick set to the top with trees; the hard granite rampart over which the compact white stream slips, and then spouts into the basin below, and the smoothly carved groove telling of the ages that have been exhausted in that merry rasping of the rock by the water-drops; the loveliness of the basin itself, when one goes down to it and contrasts its green, placid surface with the leaping crystal column that pours into it from eighty feet above,—these, and the cheerful tripping of the stream on its way again in search of new adventures, after its mad plunge, combine to make a mountain retreat, whose wildness and music Scott would have delighted to enshrine in his vigorous verse, and which no visitor of Gorham and the Glen House should leave unvisited. Trenton has not any one scene, or any one cascade, so striking. It has always seemed to me, on a smaller scale, more like the scenery at the Natural Bridge in Virginia, than any other district of the White Mountains.

About an hour is required to reach Glen Ellis Fall from the Glen House. Visitors need another hour at the spot. Generally the visit is too hurried. Twice the time that can be given is generally found to be needed.

We give next a picture of another waterfall, which is one of the most delightful resources of a visit at the Glen House. The sketch, however. is very inadequate to the subject.

"CRYSTAL CASCADE," is gained from an entrance in the woods about a mile from the Glen Ellis fall, on the way back to the Glen House, from which it is only three miles distant. It pours down from heights opposite to those which feed the Ellis river. Its descent is about eighty feet. Part of its water comes from the dome of Mt. Washington, through Tuckerman's ravine. It takes twenty or thirty minutes of forest walking and climbing to reach the Crystal Cascade. The true point to see it is not the immediate foot of the fall, although most persons go there, but a high bank opposite that overhangs the aged granite, and has plenty of the softest seats cushioned with moss a foot or more in depth. If it is wildness, and the spirit of strong, bounding, unruly life that fascinates in the spot we have just left, here it is delicate and exquisite beauty.

At Glen Ellis the whole stream pitches in one concentrated tide ; here, every pint of water is spread with charming economy to the utmost service. Some seventy feet above, we can see the brook pouring in a single stream around a bend. Then the rock broadens into a rough stairway, with easy slope, which grows wider and wider to the bottom, and down these steps the spreading water sheds its white, thin, dancing and broken sheet,

View of Crystal Cascade.

showing, now and then, through its gauzy texture, the deep green mosses clinging to the rocks which soften its own fall, and make its cool music more gentle and luscious to the ear.

A friend of ours once compared it quite happily, to an inverted liquid plume—the rill above, where the water is one stream, being the stem, and the widening, fleecy flow its nodding, graceful, feathery spray. As to the *form* of the Cascade, nothing can be finer than the simile. But the delicate texture and color of the descending rill suggest laces, and frills, and foam-embroidery. It is as though fairy milliners had set their wits to work to weave a ruffled bosom for the rocky breast of Mt. Washington, out of the snow-flax that falls in Winter around his head.

There is a youthful and masculine energy in the Glen Ellis fall. The Crystal Cascade shows rather a feminine, maidenly delicacy and grace. There are always two parties among those who visit these falls,—some contending for the superiority of the first, others for the greater charm of the last. If the reader visits both, no doubt he will adopt our opinion that neither can be spared, and that they are so different as to repel comparison. A long forenoon or afternoon should be taken to make the excursion to both spots.

We come now to speak of

"Tuckerman's Ravine,"

whose walls are visible from the Glen House. This ravine is a tremendous gulf in the southerly side of Mt. Washington. It was named in honor of Edward Tuckerman, Esq., who has been a faithful explorer of the White Mountains. He often visited the ravine, before the tide of travel turned to the eastern side of the mountains, to complete his knowledge of the Lichens and Flora of the region.

The hard, bare, thin and curling edge of the south-western wall of this ravine, as seen from the Glen House, is one of the most striking mountain lines visible from that fascinating spot. The gulf may be reached by climbing directly up the stream of the Crystal Cascade just spoken of. That stream flows through the centre of the sloping base of the ravine.

But the easier way is to follow the carriage road, for about two miles, up Mt. Washington; strike off to the left into a forest-path, cut by direction of Mr. Thompson of the Glen House, and cross two and a half miles of forest, that lie between the carriage road and "Hermit Lake."

This little sheet of water, so snugly embowered in the wilderness, would attract more attention, were it not for the frowning wall of the ravine that looms over it, and draws the eye upwards. It lies under the southeast ridge. Emerging from the woods here, we see that the ravine is of horse-shoe shape—the opposite outer cliff more than a thousand feet in height, the bottom sloping upwards towards the backward crescent wall, and the rim quite level. Explorers must climb along the centre of the gulf, by the bed of a stream, pausing every minute to gaze at the grim ramparts on either hand, and to invent, possibly, some new exclamation of amazement and awe. Facing the party, as they make their way slowly upward, will be the grand curve of the sheer precipice that lies some way off and up under the summit of Mt. Washington. It is symmetrical, seemingly, as the wall of the Coliseum.

The sight of that stupendous amphitheatre of stone when one gets near enough to appreciate it, would of itself repay and overpay the labor of the climb. It is fitly called the "Mountain Coliseum." No other word expresses it, and that comes spontaneously to the lips. The eye needs some hours of gazing and comparative measurement to fit itself for an appreciation of its scale and sublimity.

One can hardly believe, while standing there, that the sheer concave sweep of the back wall of the ravine was the work of an earthquake throe. It seems as though Titanic Geometry and trowels must have come in to perfect a primitive volcanic sketch. One might easily fancy it the Stonehenge of a Pre-Adamite race,—the unroofed ruins of a temple, reared by ancient Anaks long before the birth of man, for which the dome of Mt. Washington was piled as the western tower.

There have been land slides and rock avalanches as terrible in that ravine as at Dixville Notch. The teeth of the frosts have been as pitiless; the desolation of the cliffs is as complete; but the spirit of the place is not so gloomy as at Dixville. It is sublime rather than awful, or dispiriting. At Dixville, all is decay, wreck, the hopeless submission of matter in the coil of its hungry foes. In Tuckerman's ravine there is a grand battle of granite against storm and frost,—a Roman resistance, as though it could hold out for ages yet, before the siege of Winter, and all the batteries of the air.

Unless the season is very dry, the back wall of this mountain Coliseum will glitter with innumerable veins of water, which are called "The Thousand Streams." When one has reached the base of this curving precipice it is not a very difficult task to climb to the summit of Mt. Washington. Parties have sometimes done so, passed the night there, and returned to the Glen House the next day. Many also have visited the ravine by descending into it, with a guide, from the top of Mt. Washington. The distance from the summit of the mountain to the bottom of the gulf is about a mile.

A visit to Tuckerman's ravine in August will be the more interesting if "The Snow Arch," is formed there. In 1855 and 1856, this beautiful spectacle was to be seen. The snow is blown over from the summit of Mt. Washington by the northwest winds, in winter, and is packed in drifts of a hundred feet deep, under the walls of "The Coliseum." The streams of early Spring and Summer channel the snow bank, and it gradually melts from the roof within, till a vast snow cave is formed, through which a person may walk. In August, 1855, the snow field measured about 300 feet long, 70 in breadth, and 15 in depth. The roof of the part that was chanelled was some five feet thick, and very solid. A hatchet was necessary to cut it. The top of the span was about ten feet high inside. The whole roof was wrought into beautiful scallops and chasings by the melting and dropping of the snow within. The bank does not disappear till the last of August. The dog-day fogs penetrate and dissolve it. Thus we narrowly escape having a glacier formed near the top of Mt. Washington.

GLEN HOUSE TO THE CRAWFORD HOUSE.

Having now passed a few days, or, still better, a few weeks amidst the wondrous scenery around the Glen House, we leave with reluctance this pleasant Hotel, and its hospitable host, and continue our journey to the Crawford House, at the Great Notch.

This trip is made in stages, the route lying at first in a southerly direction through Pinkham Notch, then westerly along the south-eastern flank of the mountains, and finally at the Great Notch, passing directly through to the northern side. The distance is 34 miles, and the fare $3.00.

The same point is sometimes reached from the Glen House by *private* coaches along the north-western side of the White Hills, and over Cherry Mountain. By this route you lose the sublime impression always experienced on approaching the Notch from the south, but gain the enchanting view from Cherry Mountain. If, however, you intend proceeding from the Crawford House to Franconia, the Cherry Mountain route must be partially retraced, so that more variety is gained by selecting, for the present trip, the route through Pinkham Notch.

The stages start as soon after breakfast as the passengers can conveniently be ready. There are generally at least two vehicles, a stage-coach, and an open mountain-wagon. If you wish to enjoy an unobstructed view of the noble scenery on the route, and do not mind a shower, such as often in summer comes on very suddenly among these hills, you will not hesitate to adopt the latter airy mode of conveyance. The road lies directly down the little descent towards the south. On the right, the partially completed carriage road to Mt. Washington turns off, and crossing the rustic bridge over the Peabody River is soon lost among the trees. The forests now close in on each side, the open space of Bellow's Clearing, which we have just left, is no longer visible, and we can catch only occasional glimpses through the foliage of the overhanging cliffs of Carter Mountain on the left, and of the lofty hills beyond the river on the right. We are fairly within the portals of Pinkham Notch, and the silence and solitude are relieved only by the tinkling, and bubbling, and rushing of the Peabody River, as the road follows closely its rocky bed. Here and there are quiet pools much frequented in the warm season by the lover of trouting.

About two or three miles from the Glen House, the road crosses the river twice in quick succession, and reaches the highest point of the Notch. Here the Peabody River, and the Ellis issue in nearly parallel courses from the forest on the right, so near to each other that a slight amount of labor would turn either stream into the other. As soon as they have passed under the road, the Peabody turns abruptly down the ravine to the north to unite with the Androscoggin, while the Ellis takes an opposite course down the Notch towards the Saco.

Between the two streams, on the right, is the entrance to the Crystal Cascade, marked by roughly engraved letters on the bark of a tree. These beautiful falls are distant from the road only about a third of a mile, but are approached by an exceedingly rough path.

After leaving the entrance to this Cascade we cross the Ellis River, and soon pass the Mineral Spring House, an unfinished, and uninhabited cottage in the edge of the forest on the right. This house, the only shelter for seven miles, was located here on account of the supposed medicinal character of the spring near by, but the project has been abandoned, and the building seems going to ruin.

Proceeding a little farther we reach the entrance to Glen Ellis Falls on the left. This cascade is nearer the road than the other, and is approached by an easy path of plank.

The Foot of Pinkham Notch.

Continuing down the Notch two or three miles, the country

opens again, and cleared fields on the intervales of the Ellis River take the place of unsubdued forests. Near here a glance toward the north-west is rewarded by a fine view of a monster boulder, apparently rolling down a south-eastern spur of Mt. Washington. The first house is soon reached, and we seek to catch a sight of the inhabitants, whose nearest neighbors on the north are seven miles away. The house is quite large, and is considerably visited by artists and others, who delight in the wildness of the surrounding scenery, and the substantial mountain fare.

To this vicinity Capt. Joseph Pinkham, and four other hardy pioneers, removed in April 1790, from Madbury in the lower part of the State. The Pinkham family came up over the snow, which lay five feet deep, and brought all their household goods from Conway on a hand-sled. They found their log-cabin, which had been erected during the previous autumn, almost buried in the snow. One of the sons of the family, Mr. Daniel Pinkham, constructed the Notch road, and gave it his name.

JACKSON.

A few miles more through a widening valley brings us to a sudden turn, which discloses the white spire of the church in "Jackson City." We greet this token of returning civilization with something of the enthusiasm which a sailor feels on reaching land after a long voyage. It belongs to a Free Will Baptist Society, founded in this quiet valley as early as 1803. You should not omit, near this point, to look back at the dark gorges, which open miles away towards Mt. Washington. A few steps brings us to a nice little Inn, where the horses are changed, and passengers for Conway and Lake Winnipisaukee take another coach. Here may almost always be seen a few artists, and other guests, drawn thither by the delightful scenery, and the rural comfort of the hotel. Just at the north-east of the house is a romantic cascade on the Wild Cat Brook, a tributary of the Ellis River. While the horses are changing you will have time enough to visit these falls, and will be amply compensated for the trouble, if there is the usual quantity of water, leaping from rock to rock.

From the portico of the Hotel there is gained a fine view of the surrounding mountains. Facing the south you see Iron Mountain rising to the height of 2,900 feet on the right, and the bald peak of Tin Mountain on the left. Soon after leaving the Hotel the two noble peaks of Doublehead come into view in the northeast. The nearer peak is 3,000 feet high, and the farther a hundred feet higher. Jackson has vast mineral resources, possessing, besides many less important metals, iron, copper, and tin. The last was discovered here, before it had been found in any other part of the United States. This town was first named New Madbury, then Adams, in honor of the great statesman, and finally received it present name, when Adams and Jackson were competitors for the Presidency, all its voters but one being in favor of the latter.

Goodrich Falls.

A mile below Jackson, just before crossing the new trestle bridge over the Ellis River, you can obtain a fine view of Goodrich Falls. Leaving the road a little above the bridge, and proceeding a few rods to the right, you come to an old bridge in front of the cataract. This is the largest perpendicular fall to be seen among the mountains, and after heavy rains appears quite grand. At any time the view down the river between the steep wooded banks is exceedingly picturesque. A short scramble on the opposite side of the river will be amply rewarded by the nearer view of the Falls, which is thereby gained. The drivers on all the mountain routes are very kind and accommodating, and will readily allow time for the ramble. Indeed, we may here say, that, at all times, the tourist will find them ready to stay as long as he may desire to obtain views of the fine scenery in any part of the route. In this vicinity the traveller first notices that pleasant element of the mountain scenery, the little girls standing by the road side with tiny birch baskets filled with berries for sale. Buy some raspberries, or some blueberries, and you will make many a little heart glad, as well as secure the neat baskets as souvenirs of your trip.

Valley of the Saco.

Soon after leaving Goodrich Falls, we reach the Saco valley, and crossing the Ellis River, the Rocky Branch, and the Saco in quick succession, turn abruptly towards the west. For the remainder of the distance to the Crawford House, we are passing over the same road, as those who come up from Centre Harbor, and Conway.

At the time of the Willey slide the Rocky Branch, which here joins the Saco, rose so rapidly, as to surround a log cabin on its banks, before the inmates could make their escape. They soon found themselves floating down the swollen stream, but were at last landed in safety on the summit of a little hill.

As we proceed up the Saco, the beautiful level intervals, on each side of the stream, are worthy of our attention, as well as the hills, which rise boldly on each side at no great distance from the river. Before us, a little to the left, are the three peaks of Tremont Mountain, about 3,500 feet in height, and directly behind for a long distance we can see the noble pyramidal form of Kearsarge, sometimes called Pequawket. On its summit, at the height of 3,400 feet, is distinctly seen the large hotel, erected some years ago for the accommodation of visitors. It is now unfortunately uninhabited, and almost in ruins. The solitariness of Kearsarge gives it a lonely dignity scarcely equalled by any other mountain in the region. In this vicinity is seen an old brown house on the left hand of the road, bearing the startling announcement that a bear, a rattlesnake, and a hedgehog can be seen " hear."

The part of the Saco Valley, through which we are now passing, forms the town of Bartlett. It is nearly coincident with a tract of land granted to Capt. William Stark and Vere Royce, as a reward for services performed in Canada during the French and Indian War, and was settled about 1770. There is no compact village in the town, but the houses are scattered at considerable intervals along the valley. At one of these, which looks like a farm-house, but is also a tavern, you will stop for dinner, and will not find the well-spread table unwelcome after your long ride, nor esteem fifty cents, the ordinary charge, an exorbitant price. It is customary for every guest to register his name in the record-book in the hotel parlor, and as this is the great high road to the mountains, you will be interested in observing the names of many friends, who have preceded you on this journey.

After proceeding a short distance from the half-way house, which we have just left, we pass a high rock close to the road on the left hand, called

SAWYER'S ROCK,

and famous for its association with the discovery of the Great Notch. The story is narrated by Mr. Willey in his White Mountain Incidents, a book which should be in the hand of every traveller to this region. In early periods the land on the north side of the mountains was almost valueless on account of the long circuit, which must be made to reach it. It is supposed that the Indians had been acquainted with the pass, now called the Notch, and had taken their prisoners through it to Canada, but it was still unknown to the white inhabitants until one day about 1771, a solitary hunter, named Nash, happened to climb a tree on Cherry Mountain to look for game. Casting his eye towards the south-east he thought he perceived an opening through the mountains. Making his way in that direction, he arrived at last at the narrow opening called the Gate of the Notch, and passing through the gorge he proceeded to Portsmouth, and announced the long wished-for discovery to George Wentworth. Hunters had before scaled the mountains on foot, so the Governor determined to test the feasibility of the pass, by promising Nash a large tract of land on the north side of the mountains, since known as Nash and Sawyer's Location, if he would get a horse through and bring him to Portsmouth. This was by no means an easy task, but by the aid of Sawyer, a fellow hunter, he succeeded in bringing the horse through, sometimes drawing him up high precipices with ropes, and then letting him down on the other side. When they let him down the last rock on the southern side, Sawyer drained the rum from his bottle, and dashing it on the rock exclaimed—"This shall hereafter be called Sawyer's Rock," and so it is.

A little beyond this point the road turns to the north, as it follows the great bend of the Saco round Hart's Ledge on the opposite side of the valley, and soon crosses a small stream called Sawyer's River. At the source of this brook, three or four miles to the west is Bemis Pond, a small sheet of water, often resorted to for trouting by the guests of the Mt. Crawford House.

Nancy's Brook and Bridge.

The forests and the mountains now begin to close in, as if to prepare the traveller for the contracted atmosphere of the Notch, and a little brook comes leaping down the mountain side with a winning air of wild freedom. This is Nancy's Brook, and the rustic structure thereon across it is Nancy's Bridge. It was near this spot that a disconsolate maiden, whose name is here preserved, perished with fatigue and cold, when she had walked all the way from Jefferson through the snow and darkness in pursuit of her recreant lover. She was found stiff and cold, sitting at the foot of a tree near the bank of this book. The incident has already afforded material for the pen of the novelist, and the skill of the pencil has been repeatedly spent in portraying the picturesque beauty of Nancy's Bridge, and its setting of wild rocks, and trees, and bubbling cascades.

A half a mile beyond this bridge, we come to the Mt. Craw-

FORD HOUSE. This hotel has been in past years a favorite resort for the sportsman, and the quiet loving traveller, and once it was one of the principal public houses of the region, but during last summer it was closed. The situation is a delightful one, and it is hoped the house will again open its doors to visitors. There is a path from this point to Mt. Washington, styled the Davis Road, which is longer than the other, but inferior to none in romantic interest. We are now in the midst of Hart's Location, which borders the Notch on the southern side, while Nash and Sawyer's approaches it on the north.

On this very spot old Abel Crawford, styled the "Patriarch of the Mountains," lived and reared his family. At the age of seventy-five he made the first ascent ever made to Mt. Washington on horse-back. When he was eighty he was so robust as to think nothing of walking five miles before breakfast to his son's house at the Gate of the Notch. His son, Ethen Allen Crawford, called the "Giant of the Hills," cut the first bridle-path to Mt. Washington in 1821. He resided at that time near the Giant's Grave on the north side of the Notch, and the path was nearly, if not quite, coincident with the one now called "Fabyan's Path." All the paths on the western side of the mountains were cut by the Crawfords. Ethen was a great hunter, and used to delight his guests with quaintly related stories of many a daring adventure. Both he and his father acted as guides to the travellers, who in their time visited the mountains. At the time of the Willey Slide, the Saco rose so rapidly and so high, as to flood the lower story of Mr. Crawford's house, before the family could escape. He himself was away from home, but the rest retired to the upper story, and during the raging tempest, Mrs. Crawford stood at the north window, clearing away with a pole, the logs, and other drift, which pressed with so much force against the house, as to threaten it with instant destruction every moment. This intrepid woman was the mother of eight sons.

THE CHAPEL OF THE HILLS.

In the vicinity is a little church, built by the assistance of a benevolent lady of Boston, and consecrated January 1854. The donor was actuated to this good work by observing, in one of the Boston newspapers, a letter from a visitor to this region, setting forth its religious destitution. She immediately offered to contribute two hundred dollars towards the erection of a chapel far up among the hills, if the inhabitants of Bartlett would raise the balance. As a result of these efforts, we see this comfortable building, the only church for miles around. Like some of the little chapels in Westminster Abbey, it seems to stand in the midst of a grander and loftier temple, reared by the hand of Nature, and consecrated long ago by the prayers and the songs of the Red Man.

THE APPROACH TO THE NOTCH.

As we proceed up the Saco, Mt. Crawford, and the Giant's Stairs, are distinctly visible beyond the river on the right. The southern peak, Mt. Crawford, is 3,200 feet high, and the northern is 3,500. Between them is Mt. Resolution. Over these eminences passes the Davis Road to Mt. Washington. After crossing the Saco twice, the road now turns a little towards the northwest. This road was the tenth turnpike constructed in New Hampshire, and was incorporated in 1803. It extends through the Notch, and through Nash and Sawyer's Location twenty miles, and cost forty thousand dollars. On account of the immense travel over it, it nevertheless paid well. Before it was laid out, the common county road crossed the Saco thirty-two times, in making its way up the valley. Near here we pass through a forest of gigantic white birches, and catch an occasional view of a lofty overhanging mountain directly in front.

At last the Great Notch bursts upon our view in all its sublime majesty, and, looking up the gorge, we behold the frowning Webster on the right, the scarred sides of the fatal Willey on the left, and the rounded summit of Mt. Willard just appearing far away in the middle of the picture. This view of Mt. Webster from the end, is perhaps the most impressive way, in which it can be seen. We cannot help wondering if human foot has ever dared to tread its apparently inaccessible heights, or to explore its mysterious recesses. Well was it named for him, whose overhanging, thoughtful brow, these majestic cliffs so much resemble.

Descending rapidly into the Notch the road passes over the *debris* of the first slide, now covered with a considerable growth of white birches. Boulders are scattered around in wild confusion, and the atmosphere of death and destruction seems still to linger about the place. A few rods brings us to the second slide, and we catch the first sight of

The Willey House.

This famous edifice, situated on the left hand of the road directly under Willey Mountain, was the scene of the great disaster, which caused the loss of the whole Willey family. Only the northern and smaller portion of the present building was standing at that time, the southern part having been added in later years to accommodate guests, who sometimes stop here. The original building was erected by a Mr. Hill for a public house, not far from 1820. Previous to this period there was no habitation between the Old Crawford House, and the Rosebrooks', a distance of 13 miles. Its hospitable roof was often greeted with gratitude by many a traveller, who would perhaps otherwise have perished in the awful snow-drifts, so common in the Notch during winter. After occupying the house for a few years, Mr. Hill left it, and it stood empty for several months. At last, in the Autumn of 1825, Mr. Willey moved in with his family, and passed the ensuing winter very comfortably. In the June following, however, there was a slide from the mountain, which terrified them considerably, but did them no permanent injury. It proved to be a warning of the great disaster,

View of the Willey House.

which was to follow. On the night of Aug. 28, 1826, a most violent tempest raged about the Notch, and a vast amount of soil, and of rocks on Willey Mountain was precipitated into the valley below, overwhelming the whole family, consisting of Mr. Willey, his wife, five children, and two hired men. The house itself was not injured, but it is supposed that the inmates, rushing out in their terror, were overtaken by the slide a little lower down by the Saco. A pile of stones alone marks the place where the bodies of most of them were found. The father, mother, and two children, rest in the burial place of the family, near the boundary of Bartlett, and Conway. The house was deserted for a year after this event, but at last a family named Pendexter moved in, and it has been generally occupied since that period. Of late years it has become important as a show-place, twelve and a half cents being charged for shewing each person through the house. There is, however, nothing within the ruinous edifice of sufficient interest to warrant even this trifling expenditure. In the rear is seen the great rock, once thirty feet high, which separated the slide, and thus saved the house. The top of it is now almost level with the ground around it, and a pole thirty feet high has been erected close by. to assist the inexperienced mind in forming a correct conception of the former height of the rock. So kindly is sight-seeing here made easy for beginners. From the top of the rock, a beautiful path, quite the most attractive element of the scene, winds among the birches on the slide, far up the mountain. In front of the house is still standing the ruin of the stable, which was half demolished by the avalanche. Before re-mounting the coach you should not fail to drink some of the excellent water, to be found at the upper end of the piazza. It is sometimes wondered that any one dares to inhabit so perilous a spot as this, but it must not be forgotten that the side of Willey is now so bare, that there seems nothing more to come down but the solid rock of the mountain. On the opposite side of the river, however, Mt. Webster rises apparently perpendicular to the height of two thousand feet above the valley, and almost threatens to overwhelm it. In every tempest the inhabitants of the Willey House hear the enormous rocks crashing down its precipitous sides, with the sound of thunder, while lightnings play about its awful brow. But there is in reality no danger.

The Head of the Notch.

After leaving the Willey House the road winds up the narrow ravine for about three miles, ever and anon crossing the rushing stream, and bending around projecting rocks. This part of the trip is generally performed at the close of the day, when the lengthened shadows add a gloomy grandeur to the scene. Shut in by dismal walls 2,000 feet high, our hearts sink within us, with a feeling of utter insignificance. The steep sides of Willey Mountain are diversified by tier above tier of wandlike white birches, the stems being peculiarly apparent on account of the steepness of the mountain. At the top of this mountain on a sort of plateau, is a little lake called Ethan's pond. Near as this is to the Saco, it yet finds its outlet towards the southwest into the Pemigewasset, and so into the Merrimack. On each side far above our heads little torrents come pouring down over the rocks in cascades, which will be examined more at our leisure, in excursions from the Crawford House. As we proceed, the "Old Maid of the Mountain," a great stone face just above the road on the right hand side, and an overhanging rock on the same side, called the "Devil's Pulpit," come into view. On the face of this, with imagination, can be seen another profile, called "The Infant," and is said to have been discovered by Ex-Gov. Baker, now of Iowa. In front, far up on Mt. Willard, which has now assumed gigantic proportions, appears the black mouth of the "Devil's Den." Just before arriving at the Gate, the road turns a little to the right with a bend in the Notch itself, and we suddenly emerge from the

5*

wondrous gorge, between two chaotic piles of rocks, and uprooted trees, only twenty-three feet apart.

The Crawford House is now in sight, and a short ride over a level road brings us to the piazza. We must not be surprised at the number of spectators, who come to see our debarkment, for the arrival of the evening coaches, is one of the most exciting events of the day here.

THE CRAWFORD HOUSE AND VICINITY.

The Crawford House is a large and new edifice, very commodious and agreeable for a summer hotel. There are pleasant piazzas on the outside, and five halls, much used in the evening for promenading, run the entire length of the house within. The parlor is large and well furnished, the dining-room ample in its proportions, and its table always supplied with the delicacies of the metropolitan markets, as well as such substantial articles of mountain production, as delicious berries, and the richest milk and cream. The Office is situated in the central part of the house, and generally presents as busy a scene as the great square in a city. Hither every one comes to talk over his plans, and to make arrangements for various excursions, or for continuing his journey to other points of interest. You should be careful, *as soon as* you arrive, to book your name at this place for a horse to Mt. Washington, if you intend to make the ascent within a few days, as often all the ponies are engaged for a day or two beforehand. The price of a horse to the summit and back with guides for the party is $3. You should also book your name a day or two in advance, if you intend to secure a seat in any of the stages which leave this house, for it sometimes happens that every seat is engaged, if you wait till the time for starting. Here also is the Post Office of this wild region. Portraits of two of the Crawfords, patriarchs of these mountains, adorn the wall. The lodging rooms of the house are well furnished, and pleasant, especially those, which have windows towards the Notch. Connected with the hotel are a bowling-alley for rainy-day and evening amusement, and extensive stables, furnished with a large number of horses, to be used either under the saddle or in carriages, for the delightful rides about this vicinity. Last summer two tame bears, in the edge of the forest at the southwest of the house afforded the guests much amusement. This excellent establishment is kept by Mr. J. L. Gibb, with the assistance of his gentlemanly clerk, Mr. W. H. Witt. The price of board here, as at all the first class houses among the mountains, is $2.50 per day.

The Plateau.

We are now in the midst of a little plateau, about 2,000 feet above the sea. It is the highest point of the valley, and the water flows from it in both directions, the spring near the house discharging its contents down through the Notch into the Saco, and that at the stables emptying itself into a tributary of the Ammonoosuc, and reaching the sea through the Connecticut. In front of the house there is a beautiful fountain, and farther on a tiny lake, which forms the head water of the Saco. Down near the Gate of the Notch on the left hand is the ruins of the old Notch House. This was erected by Ethan Allen Crawford and his father, and kept for a public house by Thomas J. Crawford, a brother of Ethan. Many a thrilling tale is narrated of the adventures of early guests at this house, who attempted to ascend the mountains under the guidance of the Crawfords, or sometimes even without guides. The appearance of the Notch House is familiar to almost every one, from its having been pictured so often in Geographies and other books. It was the largest house of the region for a long time after it was built, and had the upper story project over the arch-topped sheds below in a peculiar manner. After the Crawford House was erected, the building was used for lodging the supernumeraries, who could not find quarters in the large hotel. A year or two ago the time-honored structure was unfortunately burned. About half way down the road to the Gate, on the right hand, is a guide-board pointing out the path to

MT. WILLARD, AND THE DEVIL'S DEN.

This mountain is easily ascended in carriages to the very summit, where the view down the Notch fully repays all the trouble of the ascent. The height above the Crawford House is but little more than 2,000 feet. Carriages are afforded for the excursion at a reasonable rate, whenever a party desires to make it. Near the top of the mountain on the southern side is the remarkable cavern, called the "Devil's Den," whose black mouth was distinctly seen in coming up the Notch. This was explored in August, 1856, by Dr. Benjamin Ball, of Boston, Mass. There were rumors current previous to his exploration that it extended far into the mountains and that by another opening bears sought its recesses to devour their prey. It was said to have been explored by one of the Crawfords who discovered large quantities of bones. All this must have been a myth. Dr. Ball was let down by ropes. He carried candles and a knife to defend himself from wild animals. The "Den" however, proved to be only about twenty feet wide, fifteen feet high, and twenty feet deep. It is so cold and damp that not even the birds take refuge there. The only trophies of his exploration were two hawk's feathers.

The excursion to the top of Mt. Willard, and the Devil's Den, forms one of the pleasantest features of the entertainment afforded in the vicinity of the Crawford House.

Another favorite ride or walk, is through the Gate of the Notch, about three-fourths of a mile, to the

Silver Cascade.

The stream which forms it, when first seen far up on the mountains, is about two miles from the road, and falls from that point not far from eight hundred feet, over perpendicular cliffs before reaching the Saco. By leaving the road at the bridge, you can penetrate to the foot of the fall, where the water rests at last in a quiet basin. If accustomed to climbing, you may pursue the excursion farther, and gain a closer acquaintance with the wild and beautiful cascade.

The Flume is still farther down the Notch, and is well worthy of a visit. The fall here is between two and three hundred feet. These cascades will appear to particular advantage, if you are fortunate enough to walk down into the Notch, on a moonlight evening. Carriages also, often leave the Crawford House on other excursions, such as to the Willey House, and to Ammonoosuc Falls, which will be described below.

Gibb's Falls. There is near the Crawford House a series of cascades which have been but recently discovered and are comparatively unknown, but which are well worthy of the attention of the tourist. By striking into the woods near the stables of the Crawford House and following the aqueduct which supplies the hotel with water, the traveller soon reaches a brook which presents a succession of falls that in romantic loveliness are inferior to none in the White or Franconia mountains. To the most striking of these the name of the gentlemanly and accommodating landlord of the Crawford House has been given. Gibb's Falls is about a quarter of a mile from the point at which the aqueduct issues from the brook and is easily accessible in a half hour's walk from the hotel. The water at this point makes an abrupt descent of thirty or forty feet in two distinct sheets which are separated by a projecting cliff draped in a scanty verdure of lichens and mosses and crowned by a single monster pine. The contrast between the emerald greenness of the projecting islet and the foaming torrents which encompass it on either hand is picturesque in the extreme and these hitherto nameless falls are well worthy the attention of the artist and the lover of nature. But the greatest feat to be performed during your stay at this hotel, and that for which the others are only preparative, is the ascent of Mt. Washington.

Ascent of Mt. Washington from the Crawford House.

During the height of the season the excursion is made every day, when the weather will allow, and generally occupies about ten hours. It can be made, however, in a somewhat shorter time if necessary. The distance to the Summit is, according to the guide-board at the entrance to the path, only *seven* miles, but, if you have a pleasant day, you will be by no means sorry to find it *nine*, which is commonly supposed to be nearer the truth. The entire distance is accomplished on the backs of the most sure-footed Canadian ponies, with the attendance of two or three experienced mountain-guides, who will be always at hand to set a loose shoe on your horse, or to mend a failing girth. If you do not like so long a ride on horseback, you can be carried round in a carriage by a longer route over Fabyan's Path to the foot of Mt. Washington, and can then take the ponies for the last three or four miles.* By this course however you lose all the beautiful views from the four mountains passed over on the other path. These are the most satisfactory to be obtained, when, as is often the case, the summit of Mt. Washington is clothed in mist. Sometimes the ascent is made on foot, but on account of the unparalleled roughness and steepness

* See Page 68.

of these mountain paths, this method is to most persons too wearisome for enjoyment, unless they spend a long time on the ascent and pass the night on the mountain. A flask of brandy is often considered indispensable for pedestrians, as persons often faint from fatigue. Whatever path or method you select, it is never advisable to attempt the ascent, for the first time, without a guide. Many accidents and inconveniences arise every year from the neglect of this precaution. Often you pass from the brightest sunshine below into impenetrable mists upon the summits of the mountains.

The clothing for this excursion should be of the commonest description at your command, but must be as warm as any required for winter wear. The temperature below cannot be taken as a criterion of that at the height of four thousand feet or more, where it is almost without cessation severely cold. Thick woolen mountain-jackets can be obtained at the hotel, but you will be more independent if you have garments of your own suitable for the purpose. Sacks and jackets are generally worn, even by the ladies, rather than shawls or cloaks, on account of their greater conveniences in the strong winds, which blow incessantly across the tops of the mountains. Close caps or hats secured very firmly on the head by strings are indispensable for the same reason. Half the pleasure of the excursion is often lost on account of the annoyance arising from a loose hat, continually blowing off, or from a troublesome shawl or cloak incessantly flapping in the wind, and threatening to burst every fastening. The ponies are brought to the door immediately after breakfast, and when the weather is promising, the party does not generally consist of less than twenty-five. The greater part of the guests at the hotel commonly come down to the piazza at the north-eastern end of the house to see these strange looking cavaliers, in all their grotesque costumes, set out for the mountains. The path passes directly into the forest on the east.

General View of this Range.

The first mountain which we ascend on this path is Mt. Clinton. It belongs to the great range, which extends from the Notch north-easterly to Mt. Madison, a distance of fourteen miles. The whole mountain region of New Hampshire is about forty miles square, but the name, "White Mountains," is sometimes applied, for the sake of distinction, only to this particular group of which Mt. Washington is the culminating point. The following list gives the name and height of each mountain of the range, in its order, commencing at the Notch:

Mt. Webster, -	4,000 ft.	Mt. Washington,	6,285 ft.
Mt. Jackson, -	- 4,100 "	Mt. Clay, - -	5,400 "
Mt. Clinton, -	4,200 "	Mt. Adams, -	5,700 "
Mt. Pleasant,	- 4,800 "	Mt. Jefferson, -	5,800 "
Mt. Franklin, -	4,900 "	Mt. Madison, -	5,400 "
Mt. Monroe, -	- 5,400 "		

The last three stand in the order of the Presidents for whom they were named.

One of the Indian names of these mountains was "Agiocochook," which signifies, "the place of the Spirit of the Great Forest," or, according to Judge Potter, "the place of the Storm Spirit," and another "Waumbekketmethna," alluding to the *whiteness* of the mountains. The distinctive title of "White" has always been applied to them on account of their peaks being white with snow during ten months of the year. Even in July and August the bare rocks have a greyish cast, when seen from a distance, which almost entitles them to the name of *white*. These noble hills were first visited in 1632, by a man named Darby Field.

Ascent of Clinton.

At a few rods distance from the Crawford House is the foot of Clinton, which we continue to ascend for two or three miles, until at its summit we are more than two thousand feet above the point of starting, and more than four thousand above the sea. The path lies all the way through a wild forest, and is so steep and winding that we often see the more advanced of the party through the trees almost directly above our heads. Now and then we pass a long piece of corduroy made of logs laid closely together across the way, and forming a hard, but quite rough path. At some points are cool springs of water issuing from the sides of the path, where the ponies are accustomed to rest for a moment, and quench their thirst. Occasionally the way lies through a wet gulley three or four feet deep, which has the appearance of being the bed of a small mountain stream, and after a rain spatters our garments with a plentiful quantity of mud. It is most interesting on this ascent to watch the ever changing character of the trees and shrubs in their transition from beech, and yellow birch, and sugar maple, and mountain ash, and aspen poplar, and striped maple below, to white pine, and hemlock, and white birch, and spruce, and balsam fir hung with festoons of hair-like moss high up, every sort giving way near the top to a kind of dwarf fir often so intertangled, that it is possible to walk over the tops, as over moss. Just before reaching the summit of Clinton, we pass through a region of dead trees, which are supposed to have been killed by the intense cold of 1812, and the seasons, which followed until 1816, when, it is believed, they remained frozen throughout the year, even in summer. Their trunks and branches have been bleached by the rains, and the winds, and they stand like weird giants stretching out their ghost-like arms to guard the approach to the enchanted regions above. At the height of 4,000 feet we emerge from the forest, and find above nothing but scattered firs, hiding here and there in the crevices of the rocks.

VIEW FROM CLINTON.

The path lies a little to the north of the summit of Mt. Clinton, and as we wind around it over the bare rocks, the first noble mountain view bursts upon our sight. Almost directly before us, towards the east, is the conical summit of Kearsarge, and apparently near it some little silver lakes with a blue setting of many mountains, and behind us we can discern Willard, and the other mountains around the Notch, mottled here and there with the shadows of passing clouds.

As we begin to descend to the narrow ridge, which joins this mountain to the next, we gain a view of the nearer objects beneath us. On the right, at a depth of two thousand feet, is a vast forest through which winds the Mt. Washington River, and beyond is a long range of giant hills, which, like these we are on, seem marching in solemn procession towards the great central shrine. On the left at a similar depth the Ammonoosuc is seen threading the forest, and at last finding its way to the open country in the distance. The first experience of real mountain travel is gained as we slide down the rocks, and wind along the bleak ridge, which connects Mt. Clinton with

Mt. Pleasant.

The path generally pursued passes around the southern side of this mountain several hundred feet below its summit, although there is one directly over, which the ponies by no means fancy so that it is impossible to make them take it. As we pass along the narrow path, we come to a delightful spring, where we can, if we choose, drink from a glass kept there for the purpose. It is remarkable that both men and horses always drink more upon the mountains than they do below, perhaps on account of the increased rapidity of evaporation. In the vicinity of this spring, as at other sheltered sunny spots along the path, exquisite little spring flowers, such as anemones, and bluebells, are found just opening in August. The season here resembles the Arctic summer, the snow not disappearing till July, and coming again early in September. During two months vegetation comes on with wonderful speed, and the whole cycle of growth and fructification is completed. You must not allow your pony to turn out of the beaten path to crop the tender grass, as he desires, for often serious accidents are the result of such yielding. Here, if he should lose his foot-hold you would be precipitated a great distance down the side of the mountain. Mt. Pleasant has a peculiarly rounded top, and presents a beautiful appearance at a distance, whence probably its somewhat incongruous name, compared with those of all the others of the *patriot group*. On the northern side are immense slides, which are supposed to have occurred, like most of those among the mountains, in the memorable storm of 1826. After passing around Mt. Pleasant we come to a more extended sort of plain lying at the foot of

Mt. Franklin.

This is a very irregular flattened peak about a hundred feet higher than the last, and the arduous ascent to its summit is an excellent preparation for the ascent of Mt. Washington, by which alone it is surpassed in difficulty. It is almost fearful to look up at the more advanced of our party winding along the lofty crags far above our heads, but we soon climb the rocks in safety and look down in turn upon those below us. The path passes a short distance to the northwest of the summit, but there is no danger in turning out a little way to the right, and attaining the highest point. The view thence towards the south-east is extremely grand. Far to the south appear the four beautiful peaks of Chocorua, the one to the right being higher and more conical than the rest. Thousands of feet below us stretches the interminable forest, like a carpeting of rich dark grass. The mountain on the eastern side is almost perpendicular, and as we leave it behind we can see the long scar left by a slide, which occurred one stormy night last summer.

Mt. Monroe.

We are now approaching the two majestic peaks of Mt. Monroe, which is inferior to Mt. Washington in height rather than in symmetrical beauty. We pass around the south-eastern side, several hundred feet below the summit, over what we are now prepared to consider an easy path. Far down to the right is the frightful abyss, known as "OAKE'S GULF." The other side of this ravine is formed by the same range of mountains, which farther back we observed across the wide valley approaching the central cluster. As we gaze down into its dizzy depths, and see huge rocks scattered in confusion on the bottom, and perpendicular craggy precipices forming the sides, we cannot help being impressed with a feeling of awe. Sometimes clouds are entrapped in this fathomless gulf, and whirl round and round in vain attempts to escape. On the northern side of Mt. Washington is a similar ravine called the "Great Gulf."

APPROACH TO MT. WASHINGTON.

Winding around Monroe, we gain our first view of Mt. Washington towering nearly fifteen hundred feet above us. It appears to consist of an irregular pyramidal pile of shattered brown stones, standing as steep as they can, without rolling down. Too often this long-expected view is lost on account of the almost perpetual mists which surround the summit. Before reaching the foot of the cone, we must pass over an extended plateau, which is at first quite smooth, and allows the horse to trot for a short distance. Nearer the mountain, however, it is scattered with innumerable boulders, which appear to have been deposited here at the same time that the pyramid of similar stones before us was thrown up. The path winds among these rocks, and is occasionally pointed out by small heaps of stones piled up for that purpose many years ago. This plain extends a long way to the right, and is nearly a mile above the sea. Little patches of coarse grass and small ponds are found here and there upon it. In the western part is a beautiful sheet of water called the "Lake of the Clouds," from which the Ammonoosuc issues. Leaving the path, and passing along the plain toward the east, we should come to the most wonderful of all the gorges in this region,—Tuckerman's Ravine.

ASCENT OF THE LAST PEAK.

The ascent of the cone of Mt. Washington is made, at least, by parties from the Crawford House, on the southwestern side, where the rocks appear to start almost perpendicular, although in reality less steep than on the southern side. The path appears to have been formed by rolling the great blocks and slabs of stone on each side, leaving a partially clear way between. Up this we wind slowly to the very summit. The rocks are of the most uninteresting character, consisting principally of a dull brown mica-slate. During the first part of the way, a great abundance of a delicate Alpine plant, with small white flowers is observed among the rocks. It is curious to discuss the manner in which the seeds of the plant were first brought here, for it is entirely unlike any other plant found in this part of the world. But at any rate it is here, and detracts very much from the gloominess of the scene. Higher up there is nothing but bleak bare rock. Near the top at a comparatively level place, we leave the ponies to stand shivering in the cold with nothing to eat, till we are ready to return. If you propose to pass the night on the mountain, you must have another horse sent up, when you are ready to return. The few steps which separate us from the top are easily passed over on foot, the ponies being left here merely for the convenience of the guides, so that they shall not become mingled with those from other paths. A finger on a guide-board elevated upon a pile of stones points out the path, the buildings on the summit being as yet hidden from view.

THE SUMMIT.

The acre of comparatively level surface on the top of the mountain is so completely covered with irregular angular rocks, that one can scarcely find a smooth place to stand upon. The building, which first appears in sight, is the "Tip-Top" House. This is used at present as a dining room. A little to the east, and somewhat below, is the "Summit" House, the first building ever erected on the mountain. Both of these have thick walls of the native rock, and are very low, with roofs nearly flat so as to present as little surface as possible to the fierce winds. The Summit House was erected in 1852, by the united efforts of Mr. Hall and Mr. Rosebrook, two farmers of Jefferson. It was commenced in June, and sufficiently completed towards the close of July, as to form a comfortable shelter. It is bound down to the mountain by several large cables, which pass over the top of the roof. The interior is divided into two principal rooms, each of which is heated by a stove. Around these fires the shivering guests crowd, and present about the same appearance, as travellers in January stopping to warm themselves at a country Inn. The thermometer does not perhaps indicate a temperature below 50°, but the constant wind produces the effect of even thirty degrees below that point. In the rear of the main rooms are narrow dormitories, with berths arranged along the wall, like those in the cabin of a steamboat. Above are also other "sleeping-places" separated from the rooms below by wooden slats. Every cubic inch of space within the building appears to be turned to some account. The tops of the lower rooms are *ceiled* with cotton cloth, but the sides are formed of rough stone walls, well pointed with mortar like a common cellar wall. In deep recesses are good glass windows, increasing very materially the comfort of the place. This and the "Tip-Top" House, erected some years afterwards, together form a hotel, at which we can stop as long as we choose. Neither does it seem by any means a bad one, when we consider that every foot of board, and every article of furniture has been brought several miles up these steep paths on the backs either of men or of horses. *Stone* and *water* are the only materials to be obtained on the summit, a never-failing spring of the latter being found a few rods north of the Summit House, a little down the mountain. The expense of bringing up coal, added to its original cost, makes an aggregate of $40 a ton, and all articles of food are obtained only by a corresponding outlay. We must not, therefore, be surprised at the charge of $4 a day for our board, if we choose to stay awhile. If the tourist wishes to devote his whole time to the view, a luncheon taken from the hotel will make an excellent substitute for the dinner in the Summit House. It has been proposed to erect a first class hotel on the summit, and to connect it with the base of the mountain by a regularly graded road. Perhaps then the accommodations would be better, and the price lower, but there would be little to satisfy the love of adventure in ascending Mt. Washington over a Macadamized road, in a cushioned omnibus! It is by no means to be lamented, by those, who enjoy the present method of ascent, that the project has been abandoned for the present.

There are generally three parties arriving on the summit every day, one from the Crawford House, one over Fabyan's Path, and one from the Glen House. Quite a large number is generally stopping here, so that it is not unusual to meet a hundred people on the top of the mountain in the middle of the day. One of the pleasantest elements of the excursion is the manner in which so many persons are thrown for one time into one family sympathizing in their common elevation above the rest of mankind.

The view from the summit has already been described. After remaining about two hours on the summit, we must prepare for

The Descent.

Returning to the spot, where the ponies were left, we find each one looking for his steed, and mounting with as much speed, as the chilly wind, and the rough rock will allow. The ladies generally walk down the first steep descent to the plain, as it is much more difficult than the ascent. There is really no danger however, as the ponies never take a step till they see where they are going. The view is also much finer going down, as our faces are now turned away from the steep side of the mountain. Especially is it beautiful on the right of Mt. Monroe, where we can trace the silver water of the Ammonoosuc in its windings through the forest far below. Soon after reaching the plain the party becomes scattered, and we wander on perhaps alone, greeting each solitary peak, like an old friend, as we pass it, and arrive at last at the summit of Clinton. The descent of this mountain becomes somewhat tiresome, with its interminable "corduroys," and its troublesome black flies, and we are not sorry at last to discover the white piazza of the Crawford House appearing through the trees.

ASCENT OF MT. WASHINGTON BY THE CARRIAGE ROAD.

Besides the regular bridle-path up the mountain from Gibb's, there is an excellent and commodious carriage road, easily accessible from Gibb's and from Brabrook's. Few who ascend the mountain are aware of its existence, and very few of those who are aware of it, are at all familiar with the facilities thus presented for an easy and expeditious mode of overcoming the difficulties of the mountain travel.

It strikes off from the main road about half way between Gibb's and Brabrook's and follows up a branch of the Ammonoosuc. It is quite level, and, in fact, a much better road than many a one traversed by coaches every day. Any one can drive a two-horse team to "Cold Spring," which is only three miles from the summit. Stables have been erected here, and ponies for the remainder of the journey are now to be taken. From this point the ascent is directly up the side of Mt. Washington, and is perhaps steeper than the other track. But it has none of that disagreeable, tireseme corduroy road. One place which they call "Jacob's Ladder," to a white cravat, and the "Devil's," to men who patronise the guide's flask, is exceedingly steep. But the guides, when belated, always take this path.

The view on the ascent, though perhaps less extended than on the longer path, is still very pleasing. On the one hand is the wild, foaming Ammonoosuc, which rolls merrily along over rapids and cataracts or stretches in broad, gravelly reaches across your path ; on the other hand the wooded heights stretch gently up the sides of Mt. Washington with many an enchanting view down the sloping vales.

Crawford House to Profile House.

This trip, like the last, is performed in stages, which leave the Crawford House every morning about eight. The distance is not far from twenty-seven miles. If you expect to proceed through Franconia to Plymouth, and thence by rail, you had better procure tickets for the whole stage route through to Plymouth. There is an agent at the Crawford House, who will sell you such tickets for $5. If you prefer a ticket to the Flume House, five miles beyond the Profile House, it will cost you $3. It is fifty cents less to the Profile House. There are also stages leaving the Crawford House for Littleton, and the Connecticut River railways, without stopping at Franconia.

After leaving the Crawford House, we descend into the forest towards the northwest, in which we continue for several miles. Occasionally an opening in the trees on the right discloses the giant forms of the White Mountains, and in one place we observe the road turning to the right, over which carriages from the Crawford House pass in order to reach Fabyan's Path. At last we cross the Ammonoosuc, about four miles from the Notch, and arrive at the Clearing, in which is

The Giant's Grave.

This is a singular tumulus, rising sixty feet high in the midst of an extended cleared plain. From its summit there is gained a magnificent view of the surrounding mountains. Towards the east we behold Mt. Washington with all its noble compeers in their order, on each side. The monster slides on Mt. Pleasant have been imagined to resemble an Indian Chief with a plume in his cap, and a tomahawk in his hand. This resemblance is quite striking, and improves as we proceed farther and farther away. When, however, we attempt to see his squaw sitting by the Chief's side, a much larger draught on the imagination is required. But whether we recognize these resemblances or not, the lengthened scars themselves, a thousand feet in height, form a sufficiently engaging object of attention.

Grand as is the view from the Giant's Grave, we need not leave it with such reluctance, as we should, were we not to carry the picture with us for hours, as we ascend the hills to Bethlehem. On the top of this mound a remarkable echo is heard, when a horn is blown. Almost directly opposite the Giant's Grave is the ruin of Fabyan's "Mt. Washington House," which was for several years the most famous hotel of this region, but was at last unfortunately burned. From this point proceeds Fabyan's Path to Mt. Washington. It is the oldest of all the bridle paths, and was cut in 1821, by Ethan Allen Crawford, who resided at the Rosebrook house near this place. For nearly seven miles it proceeds over a comparatively level surface, till it comes to the very foot of Mt. Washington.

White Mountain House.

About half a mile farther we come to this hotel, on the site of the old Rosebrook House, and kept at present by Mr. G. T. Brabrook. It is a very pleasantly situated, and quiet House in the midst of an open tract of country. In the rear is a fine view of the White Mountains, and in front, beyond the Ammonoosuc, rises the lofty range which connects the Great Notch with Franconia.

From this house a good carriage-road has been built during the last season to within about two miles of the summit of Mt. Washington. A carriage runs over the road daily, in the season of travel. Ponies are taken for the last two miles. The price is the same as on the other routes. This is, undoubtedly, the easiest and most leisurely way of making the ascent; but while you escape the fatigue of the longer bridle-paths you also loose many of the noble views which are thereby gained.

A carriage road has also been built to the summit of Mt. Prospect, to which excursions are frequently made. This is also an excellent starting place for excursions along the Ammonoosuc. Mr. Brabrook has horses ready at all times for the accommodation of his guests. The price of board is here $2 per day.

Ammonoosuc Falls.

A short distance farther, on the left of the road, are the famous falls of the Ammonoosuc. This stream is said to be the wildest and most rapid of all the rivers of New Hampshire, falling more than a mile in its course of thirty miles, from Mt. Washington to the Connecticut river. It has many cascades, some of which are higher than this, but none more attractive. Here the water issues from a forest of evergreens, and leaps down thirty feet over broad steps of granite. The rocks on each side seem laid in courses, as if by the hand of a mason. When the amount of water is large it rushes into the pool below with such force as to throw it into heaps several feet in height. This cascade unites the wildness of Nature with a close resemblance to the nice workmanship of Art, in a most surprising and beautiful manner. It is so near the road that it is not necessary to leave the coach in order to enjoy its full effect; although one might pass several hours very pleasantly in a ramble along the banks of the river.

Ammonoosuc Bridge.

After proceeding several miles with the Ammonoosuc on our right, we suddenly cross it by a strong wooden bridge. The history of the bridges, which have been erected here, as narrated by Mr. Willey, is somewhat interesting. When Bethlehem was first settled in 1790, under the name of Lord's Hill, Capt. Rosebrook cut a road from his house through the forest about twelve miles to the new settlement. A log bridge was thrown across the river, which was however soon washed away by the spring freshets. At last the newly formed town of

Bethlehem voted in 1800 to build a bridge at this place at a cost of $390. There was such a scarcity of provisions at this time, that the workmen were forced to live on milk porridge.

BETHLEHEM.

Two or three miles over gently rising ground brings us to Bethlehem, a beautiful airy village, about seventeen miles from the Notch, famous for its view of the whole range of the White Mountains. You feel a greater satisfaction in surveying them from this place, than from any other point, where the view is so comprehensive. Towards the north west are some noble white marble mountains in Vermont, appearing clothed in a garment of snow from base to summit. This place has grown from the little settlement of "Lord's Hill" of seventy years ago, into a flourishing village containing two fine churches, five large saw-mills, and one or two extensive starch factories.

FIRST VIEW OF FRANCONIA.

From Bethlehem there are two roads to Franconia Notch. Whichever we take, we must ascend a high and toilsome hill, but the view from the summit repays us for all our delay. Directly in front appears the grand range of the Franconia Mountains, with the head of Lafayette standing majestically above them all, and on the right of it the dark opening of the Notch. This view will be described more fully hereafter.

We are now obliged to descend from our lofty position into the valley of the south branch of the Ammonoosuc, which we cross and begin the slow ascent to the Notch. Winding through its shady ravines we come at last to the Profile House.

FRANCONIA NOTCH AND ITS NEIGHBORHOOD.

The Franconia Range of hills though properly belonging to the White Mountain Range, is still so distinct and peculiar in its character as to deserve a lengthened notice. The beauties of the surrounding scenery entitle it to all the admiration which the tourist bestows upon it. Indeed by old *habitués* of the region, Franconia is considered the gem of the mountains. There is not the overpowering grandeur, which belongs to the White Mountains, while the greater variety of interesting objects amply compensates for the absence of more stately scenes. The quiet beauty, and the repose of Nature in the Franconia Notch may well introduce the traveller to the higher sublimity beyond, or refresh him as he retires from the powerful influence which he has felt before the majesty of the North. There is a tranquility in the former feeling, and a sense of relief in the latter, which prepares or soothes the mind. Here is rest; here is comfort. Beneath the shadow of these solemn mountains, the weary soul finds a calm composure. Selfishness and worldliness are rebuked. The most thoughtless are hushed to reflection, and a better understanding of life grows up in the midst of Nature's grand instructions. We do not suppose our tourist is in quest of mere pleasure; we believe him to be a better and nobler man or woman than to spend his days thus. He is open to every good influence, that will make life more rich and beautiful and fair. There is no better influence than that of which he will be sensible, in the still retreat of Franconia.

The Profile House, a new and large hotel of the very best and most comfortable accommodations, is situated in the immediate vicinity of Echo Lake, Cannon Mountain, Eagle Cliff, The Profile, and Mount Lafayette. It is on a level plain, a few acres in area, in the bosom of the hills. It has two approaches, on the north, from Bethlehem and Littleton, on the south, from the Flume House and the Pemigewasset Valley. Of the approach from Littleton we have already written. From Bethlehem, over the road from Crawford's, the approach is sometimes startling in its effect. The views shift with great rapidity, at one time are wholly concealed, at another break forth upon the traveller with surprising abruptness. Going up the slow ascent of the tedious hill east of Bethlehem, one may think it tiresome and dull, and that the vaunted glories of the region exist only in the imagination of the admirer. But on reaching the top of the hill a magnificent prospect stretches before him. Across the Franconia valley rise the lofty summits of Lafayette, with his seamed and scarred sides, and the kindred mountains, standing like sentinels to guard the pass against profane intruders. Their irregularity is most picturesque, while, at the same time, they are most finely grouped. They stand out in most august proportions, relieved by the dark blue of the clear summer sky. We ride down the hill into the twilight stillness of the forest between us and our destination, with something of reverence and awe mingled with the transports of our admiration.

Echo Lake.

In the woods, to the north of the hotel, a short distance from the road, over which we have just travelled, lies embosomed, Echo Lake. It is a sheet of water of great depth and transparency, and as it sleeps there in its secure repose, seems the very type of rest. All around rise the green hills of the region, Lafayette lifting his rocky summit high above them all. The setting is appropriate for this exquisite gem. One never wearies of the quiet scene. A little boat with paddles conveys the passenger to the middle of the Lake, and to the different points where the best views may be obtained. Here are the centres of the most marvellous echoes. The sounds of a tin horn, blown with skill, will be returned in oft repeated notes like the sweetest music. The human voice, shouting distinctly, will be re-echoed with wonderful effect, as though the invisible inhabitants of the hills were holding a colloquy with "the babbling gossip of the air." The report of a cannon fired on the shore will reverberate like peals of thunder among the fastnesses of the mountains. In the stillness of morning or in the quiet of the evening at the sunset hour, the Lake is the resort of those who best know and can appreciate the wonder of the place. The wind is whist; the waters sleep; the mountains are silent;

the purple glow is on all the trees and rocks. Then is the time to wake the slumbering echoes, and hear the many voices that reply. He that has not visited this lovely spot at this bewitching time, does not understand half the magical, secret beauty which lingers around Echo Lake.

Eagle Cliff.

Almost directly overhanging the hotel, on the north, is Eagle Cliff. It is a huge, columnar crag, separated from the crest of the mountain, and rising, perpendicularly, with jagged rocks, seemingly ready to topple from its place in wide-spread ruin beneath. This precipitous cliff derives its name from the fact that it was chosen for an eyrie by a pair of eagles a few seasons ago. They are sometimes to be seen circling around its summit, and looking down, as though with lordly disdain, upon the gazing crowds below, who have invaded their solitude. No prouder position could be chosen for a habitation by this noble bird. It stands out in the picture a most prominent and majestic peak. Approached from the south, it is finely portrayed upon the background of the sky. A point about three-fourths of a mile distant, upon the border of Ferrin's pond furnishes the finest view. Its lofty crags are distinctly seen within a frame-work of deep green, formed by the luxuriant birches and vines that attempt to clamber up its sides. At sunrise or sunset, when all is dark in the valley, the rosy light softens the rude outline, and it shines out in clear brightness above the mists below. As you sit on the piazza of the hotel, the cliff looms before you in gigantic proportions, a study for the present, and a glorious memory for the future to recall.

Profile Mountain.

Directly opposite Eagle Cliff, on the south side of the Notch, rises Cannon, or, as we prefer to call it, Profile Mountain. The former name is given, on account of a supposed resemblance to a cannon, which a rock upon its summit exhibits. The latter more appropriately belongs to it, since it bears upon the southern extremity of its crest, the "Great Stone Face." The mountain is easy of ascent, by means of a foot-path, which seems to lead almost directly from the front of the hotel to the summit. The view from the platform of denuded rock above, down the valley of the Pemigewasset surpasses description. The silvery stream, the quiet forests, the verdant meadows, the placid lakes, the clustering villages, unite in a picture of enchanting loveliness. The surrounding peaks, and the towering heights of Washington and its peers, with the softly swelling hills sloping away to the south, present all that one can imagine of the grand and of the beautiful in mountain scenery. A visit to Franconia is incomplete without the ascent of Profile Mountain. An outlay of a few dollars would complete an excellent saddle-path to its summit.

CASCADE.

Immediately behind the Profile House there is a cascade, which, from the facility with which it may be reached by the tourist, deserves our notice. A path, entering the woods in the rear of the old Lafayette House, and following the aqueduct which supplies the hotel with water, conducts us in a short and pleasant walk to a brook, which, when swollen by a recent rain, presents a succession of cascades that will amply repay a visit. The bed of the brook lies for a long distance over a shelving ledge of sufficient extent to impress one adequately with the gigantic frame-work of our granite hills. This feature of the scene, together with the charming glimpses of Echo Lake and the surrounding mountains which are caught in the ascent, will render a visit to this cascade pleasant at any time. But only after a heavy rain, or amid melting snows, is it seen to advantage, and one will often desire some such arrangement for displaying its magnificent capabilities as exists, to credit Mr. Curtis' Lotus-Eating, at the Catskill Falls.

MT. LAFAYETTE

is but five hundred feet below Mt. Washington in height, and the view from its summit, is thought by many to equal, and even surpass that from its rival's crest. A good foot-path leads up its rocky sides, and the persevering lover of nature, who is not afraid to make exertion, and is willing to expend his strength, will be most abundantly rewarded for his labors. At one time horses were kept in readiness at the hotel stables for the ascent of this lofty peak, but for some unknown reason they have not been used of late. It is to be hoped, that the enterprising proprietors of the hotels will "organize" some permanent arrangement for the convenience of the numerous visitors, who would desire to enjoy the prospect afforded them from the summit of this mountain.* "Lafayette is distinguished over its fellows," says a recent writer upon the charms of this region, "not only by his height, but also by the rocky bareness of his peaked summit, that descends with converging rows of ravines, and hemlock-topped cliffs into an immense verdant basin presented toward us. In fine weather, the dry rocks of these ravines shine like bars of silver, and after heavy rains, they glisten with the torrents disappearing into the vast shadowy basin below." There is upon the mountain, located on one of its most inaccessible points, a strange looking stone of large size and unusual form. It was named by those who discovered it, "The Altar," from a fancied resemblance which they discerned to the old Runic remains of a similar character. It is based upon a granite pile, and seemingly intended for purposes of sacrifice. It is more than probable, that it may have been used by some Indian "medicine-man" in his solitary incantations and rites. We might well imagine, how he would separate himself from his tribe, and spend the day upon the summit of this lonely peak, offering upon the altar, his sacrifice to the

* We are informed that the present enterprising company, owning the Hotels, has made arrangements to have the bridle-path re-graded, and that ponies will be furnished for those wishing to ascend. The ascent can be made in about three hours. The price for pony and guide is $3.00.

Gods whom he worshipped. The mountains have always been sacred places. Olympus has its classic fame as the seat of Jove; Sinai, Horeb, and Carmel have their Divine associations; Olivet is held in affectionate veneration, as there seem to linger even yet among its wooded heights, the accents of the Saviour's voice of prayer. Lafayette might well awe the rude worshippers of the forest and the wild, and teach them of the presence of the Great Spirit.

But the great marvel and pride of this region is the

PROFILE.

As we walk down the road to the south of the hotel, we soon come to a rude bench by the way side, and, attracted by the guide board above it, inscribed with the single, simple word, "Profile," as we direct our eyes to the point which it indicates, the huge face with all its features thoroughly delineated, stands out in bold outline, before our sight. There it is, a collossal, completely symmetrical profile, looking down upon the valley from its lofty height, perfectly distinct and clear. The tourist may possibly think that this, like other wonderful stories of which veracious Guide-books tell, may be a myth, and that the similarity may exist only in the fancy of the writer. But no! This time, at least, he will acknowledge, that there is no delusion. Nature has carved out, with the most accurate chiselling, this astonishing sculpture. Every portion of the face is there, upon the solid mountain steep. There is the stern, projecting, massive brow, as though stamped with the thought and wisdom of centuries. The nose is straight, finely cut, and sharply outlined. The thin, senile lips are parted, as though about to utter the thunders of majestic speech. The chin is well thrown forward, with exact proportionate length, betokening the hard, obstinate character of the "Old Man," who has faced, with such unmoving steadiness, the storms of ages. The Sphynx of the Desert must acknowledge its inferiority to this marvellous face upon the mountain. When seen in the morning, as the mists float up from the valley beneath and along its ponderous features, it looms into larger proportions still, and with the heavy gray beard, which sometimes settles upon its chin, and down its breast, it seems like the face of some hoary patriarch of antiquity. We think that it is Henry Ward Beecher, who makes the remark, that "as men are accustomed to hang out before their shop doors certain signs, to designate their respective occupations, so here God has sculptured this great Face, to show that in these regions, he makes MEN."

"It is not advisable," says one of the admirers of the Old Man of the Mountain, "to go to take your first look at him, when the sun lights up the chasm of his granite cheek, and the cavernous mystery of his bent brow. Go to him, when, in the solemn light of evening, the mountain heaves up from the darkening lake its vast wave of luxuriant foliage. Sit on one of those rocks by the road side, and look, if you can, without awe, at the Granite Face, human in its lineaments, supernatural in size and position, weird-like in its shadowy mystery, but its sharp outline wearing an expression of mortal sadness, that gives it the most fascinating interest." It was doubtless an object of veneration to the aboriginal inhabitants. Various traditionary tales are yet extant, respecting the superstitious homage once paid to it by the Indian tribes who frequented the locality. Relics of their life, and singular utensils of a former generation have been found near it. To the whites, however, it has been little known, till within the last forty years. In the early part of the present century, the road that passes along this way was laid out, and in clearing the land of the trees that impeded the path, the profile was discovered. Since that time, it has been an object of the most absorbing interest. The genius of Hawthorne has embalmed it in our literature, and his story of "The Great Stone Face," can only be read appreciatively beneath its shadow. We give a view of the "Old Man." It does not, however, do justice to his venerable appearance, and the traveller will find the reality for excelling the image.

View of the Old Man of the Mountain.

To those who are curious in exploration, the opportunity is easily improved of ascending by a foot path to the point above the Profile. It has been ascertained, that the height of the old man is very nearly fifteen hundred feet above the level of the little lake below it, and that the length of the face is from sixty to eighty feet. In the many conflicts with the elements which it has endured, it has been roughened and scarred. But from the road, no such appearance is presented, except through a telescope, and the face appears fair and smooth. The precipice, of which it forms the extremity, is not unlike the Palisades in appearance. It extends for nearly two miles along the escarpment of the mountain, and is a prominent part of the scenery of the section. The Profile itself undergoes many changes according to the point of observation. It changes from its severe facial outline to a jagged, and, apparently shapeless mass of rocks, or to a face with flat forehead, or with a huge, Roman nose, or to the unmeaning, and retreating countenance of some wild animal. It is only at the place where the guide-board is erected, that the Profile is to be most distinctly seen. One can spend an hour or two no more profitably than by gazing upon its fascinating, and wonderful lineaments, and he will return to look upon it once more, that it may be the last remembrance, ere he bids farewell to this delightful spot.

Profile Lake.

Immediately below the Face, as though Nature would provide for her creation an appropriate mirror, nestles the beautiful sheet of water, known as Ferrin's Pond. Why not call it by a better and more appropriate name? Let it be baptized Profile Lake, or, if one desires a more fanciful title—The Old Man's Mirror. The more prosaic call it, the Old Man's Washbowl! By whatever name it may be called, no appellation will ever detract from, or add to its simple loveliness. It lies there, surrounded by rich rolling forests, and above it the precipitous mountain! Its crystal depths reflect the overhanging trees, and its bright expanse smiles joyously in the sunlight. The very finest trout live in its waters, as though only the choicest and most delicate of fish were suited to inhabit such a pure abode. We cannot help thinking, how the Greek love of the beautiful would have peopled all this region with the creations of its sacred mythology. Even the cold fancy of occidental nature, warms beneath the genial influence, and breaks forth in the most demonstrative admiration.

Proceeding along the road, to the southward of the Profile House, about three and a half miles distant from the Hotel, we arrive at

The Basin.

The waters of the Pemigewasset, flowing from Profile Lake, after tumbling in many a beautiful cascade over the rocks that lie in their course, find their way with many meanderings, to this point near the road side. Here they fall over a rocky ledge, a few feet in height, into a deep hollow in the solid granite. The diameter of this rocky basin, formed by the continual action of the water and mingled stones and boulders from above, is about thirty feet in its shortest width, and forty feet in its longest. Its circumference is not far from sixty feet. Its depth is of such proportions—ordinarily of fifteen feet—as to form a by no means shallow bowl, which is always filled with cold, pure, and pellucid water. On one side, the rocks jut over the mimic depths, forming a dam for the flowing stream, thus producing the most exquisite of waterfalls. The embankment surrounding it, is covered, in the proper season with green mosses and sweet flowers, with their delicate bells

"Tolling their perfume on the passing air."

At the other extremity, where the delivered waters, free from their temporary imprisonment make their way out, singing as they go, is a fissure in the rock, forming another little water fall. Upon one side is a peculiar conformation of the granite, which by a slight stretch of the fancy, can be said to resemble a titanic leg and foot, scooped out and polished by the overflowing current. As you look down into these transparent waters, the bed of the Basin can be distinctly seen, so fair and clear is their emerald purity. One is almost tempted to fling aside his outer garments, and plunge into this luxurious and delicious bath. It is certainly fit for the ablutions of a goddess. There is a peculiar and almost magical charm about the Basin, which enchains you to its margin, and will not let you go free. You are obliged at last to tear yourself away with many regrets that the time of your sojourn amid these beautiful haunts of Nature is so brief. But

"A thing of beauty is a joy forever,"

and your recollection will often recur to these distant scenes, as you live over again in delighted memory, the joys of other days.

Cascades.

A rude bridge of logs is thrown across the brook at the outlet of the Basin, more for purposes of convenience, than as an enhancement of the beauty of the spot. Crossing this, and following up the stream, for about two hundred rods, one discovers a cascade of the very sweetest loveliness. The waters fall over the rocks in beautiful sheets of foam, and, with the banks lined with the richest foliage, the little stream goes on its way rejoicing. The majority of travellers do not explore this region, but are contented with a passing glance at the Basin. The best way to enjoy these scenes, is to ramble about at one's own sweet will, and meet with surprises at every step, as Nature presents her pictures. Let no one forget to examine the course of the little stream now before him. He will find all along its way, the most numerous objects to give him pleasure and satisfaction.

A mile or two farther, and we reach the

Flume House.

No site can be more full of beauty, than that, which is occupied by this commodious hotel. Directly in front is Mt. Liberty, with its fancied resemblance to the profile of Geo. Washington, closing the view of the "forest primeval," with its shades of rich green foliage, its quiet groves, and its soft and pleasant paths. On the north is the picturesque Notch, with all its surroundings in bold outline. From the southern piazza, the whole Pemigewasset valley is in sight, unequalled for the variety which the wide prospect exhibits. No one can sit on this piazza at the close of day, to watch the glories of the sunset, and note the charming effects produced on "hill and dale, and pleasant intervale," without becoming a more kindly and better man. The sweet voices of Nature are to his soul full of gratitude and praise.

The Flume and the Cascades.

In the neighborhood of the Flume House, are the three chief remaining objects of interest at the Franconia mountains. These are the Flume, the Cascade and the Pool. The former is in a south easterly direction from the hotel, about three quarters of a mile distant. A good road leads to the lower part of the Cascade below the Flume. Thence, a foot path leads up the course of the stream. Crossing and recrossing at intervals, clambering up the sides of steep rocks, again following the bed of the stream itself, one finds at every forward movement, something to admire. The cascade is a continuous fall—a sheet of molten silver, on the smooth and polished rock—of more than six hundred feet. The descent is very gradual, with occasional abruptness. With the murmur of its waters in the ear, and its marvellous beauty in the eye, we ascend to the Flume itself. No more wild and striking view can be imagined. For seven or eight hundred feet and more, the stream pours its volume along a rocky bed, which breaks it up into numberless waterfalls, between two mural precipices, that lift themselves on either side, crowned with the abundant foliage of the forest. The height of these walls, in from sixty to seventy feet. The width between them is a general average of twenty feet, except at the upper end. Here the walls approach each other. Suddenly contracting to about ten feet, they hold suspended between them, about mid way up their sides, a huge boulder of granite. So nicely is it adjusted, and so slight appears its hold, that one would think the slightest touch sufficient to push it from its resting place into the ravine below. By what process it has fallen into its present position—indeed in what manner this remarkable fracture of the rock has taken place—is a puzzle for scientific heads. Its presence greatly adds to the wildness of the scene. We are content with that, and do not care to speculate about its cause. In general, one can follow the stream through this narrow gorge—not without trepidation as he passes beneath the suspended mass—and by climbing the rocky heights, can obtain a capital view from above. The trunk of a tree lies across the chasm, forming a temporary and precarious bridge. We would suggest to the proprietors of the hotels, to fell one or two more trees, and give a safer foot-hold to those adventurers, who are desirous of seeing all the wonders of the place. In the Autumn, when the forests are rich in purple, crimson, and gold, or in the winter, when the ravine is filled with snow, and icicles hang from the cliffs, and the little stream bursts through its partial confinement, the scene must be one of great grandeur. In the luxuriance of summer, it is more fresh and glowing, the verdure of the woods relieving the nakedness of the rocks. In all seasons, it is a place for study, for reflection and delight.

The scene most forcibly suggests to one the following lines from Shelley's Cenci, (Act 3, scene 1). It would seem as if the Poet had in mind the Flume itself. It is the speech of Beatrice when they are plotting the destruction of Count Francesco.

"But I remember
Two miles on this side of the fort, the road
Crosses a deep ravine; 'tis rough and narrow,
And winds with short turns down the precipice;
And in its depth there is a mighty rock,

View of the Flume.

Which has, from unimaginable years,
Sustained itself with terror and with toil
Over a gulf, and with the agony
With which it clings, seems slowly coming down;
Even as a wretched soul hour after hour
Clings to the mass of life; yet, clinging, leans;
And, leaning, makes more dark the dread abyss
In which it fears to fall: beneath this crag
Huge as despair, as if in weariness,
The melancholy mountain yawns—below,
You hear but see not an impetuous torrent
Raging among the caverns, and a bridge
Crosses the chasm; and high above there grow,
With intersecting trunks, from crag to crag,
Cedars, and yews, and pines, whose tangled hair
Is matted in one solid roof of shade
By the dark ivy's twine. At noonday here
'Tis twilight and at sunset blackest night."

Returning from the Flume, we find the path to the

Pool

directly in front of the Hotel, leading straight into the woods. A walk of three quarters of a mile, beneath the overhanging branches brings us to this famous and wonderful formation. A deep excavation, as though hewn by human hands, in the granite, holds the waters, which enter by a cascade from the upper, and escape through an opening in the mass of rocks at the lower extremity. The width of the Pool is about a hundred and fifty feet; its depth about forty feet. From the brink of the wall above to the surface below, the distance is very nearly one hundred and fifty feet. It is a place of wondrous attraction. It may not have the charm of the Basin, but it is more secluded, and the sight of it is an ample reward for the toils of the way, if toils they may be called. The rambling wood path and the stroll along its pleasant way can never be toilsome to the true lover of Nature, even though so worthy an object of admiration as is the Pool, were not at its termination.

HOTELS.

We cannot close our notice of this locality, without recommending to the tourist the comforts and conveniences of the two Hotels, which are established here. Both are unsurpassed in their character. If faithful attention, clean rooms, — such as Isaac Walton loved — a profuse table, and beauty of locality, can furnish a desirable resting place for the traveller, these are all to be found in this favored spot. The Houses are under the management of one Company, styled "The Flume and Franconia Hotel Company." Their property embraces the two Hotels with their out-buildings, horses, carriages, etc., and about fifteen hundred acres of land. The Company is chartered by the State and the property is valued at $150,000. The Directors are well and favorably known in the business world; Hon. JOSEPH A. GILMORE of Concord has been chosen President. The mere mention of his name is a sufficient guarantee that these Hotels will maintain their long established reputation.

The Profile House is under the sole direction of HIRAM BELL, Esq., whose reputation, as a landlord, is second to none. Large experience and a perfect knowledge of the mountains and of the wants of travellers has gained for Mr. Bell a reputation, which, we are confident, future seasons will extend.

The Flume House is under the superintendance of W. H. DUNTON, Esq., long and favorably known in northern New York. The "Flume House" has always been a favorite tarrying place for those accustomed to spend a long time among the mountains. In a small chapel, near by, religious services are commonly held on Sunday.

Long may these Hotels continue in prosperity and success, to be remembered by the sojourner under their roofs, with grateful and pleasing recollection!

NOTE. We cannot too strongly recommend the necessity to the tourist of sufficient and water proof clothing. The weather is so uncertain among the mountains, that it is well to be prepared to defy the elements. The coolness of the atmosphere renders extra clothing necessary, while rubber boots, capes for ladies, and overcoats for gentlemen will enable one to enjoy the scenery whatever aspect the face of the sky may wear.

Having now completed the circuit of the mountain region, the traveller may retrace his steps to Bethlehem, and, taking the cars at Littleton, may return home by any of the various routes hereafter described. Or he may proceed through the lovely valley of the Pemigewasset to Plymouth, and thence by cars to Boston, visiting Lake Winnipisaukee on the way.

We propose now to give the more detailed account of the routes *to* the White Mountain region.

ROUTES FROM NEW YORK TO BOSTON.

I. New York to Boston, via Stonington and Providence; on Long Island Sound by Steamboat to Stonington; thence to Providence and Boston by rail, arriving at Boston at 5 o'clock, A. M. Fare $4.00

The Steamers Plymouth Rock and C. Vanderbilt, leave their pier at New-York late in the afternoon, making the passage to Stonington in seven hours, and in less time, with favorable tides. These boats are universally acknowledged to be the safest, most comfortable, and quickest upon the sound, and the Stonington route is deservedly popular. The Sound boats all follow the same channel, and consequently, the same views are presented from all. At one o'clock, A. M., a safe arrival is made at Stonington, where a train is in waiting for the immediate conveyance of passengers to Boston.

Stonington is a busy place, engaged to a considerable extent in the whale and other fisheries. Its hardy sailors are to be found all over the world, and its ships are generally successful.

Thence the road passes through the entire State of Rhode Island in a diagonal direction. The towns of Westerly, Charlestown, South Kingstown, North Kingstown, East Greenwich, and Warwick, lie along the route. Rhode Island is filled with manufacturing villages, whose names it is not necessary to give. Wherever there is a stream powerful enough to turn a water wheel, there will quickly be found a little mill, the centre of a hamlet. No State in the Union is so industrious in proportion to its size. Small, but smart, is "Little Rhody."

PROVIDENCE is one of its capitals, for, like her sister State, Connecticut, and for a similar reason, Rhode Island has two capitals, and is equally well governed. Providence is the wealthiest city in New England, according to its size, with possibly the exception of New Bedford. If its public spirit were commensurate with its wealth, it would be the handsomest city in its section of the country. But it has no City Hall, the State House is an inferior building, and is used as a Court House during the recess of the General Assembly, and the Churches are inexpensive structures of clumsy architecture. It contains some elegant private residences upon the high land on the easterly side of Providence river, where also are situated, commanding a fine and wide prospect, the buildings of BROWN UNIVERSITY. A celebrated School, under the direction of the Society of Friends, and an Asylum for the Insane are also located here. The United States Government has recently erected a substantial granite building, for the uses of the Post Office, Custom House, and the United States Courts, furnishing accommodations for these purposes, not surpassed in the country. Nowhere in the United States are the streets kept in so good order, or so well lighted as in Providence, and no place is more orderly and quiet. On a bright day the city presents a brilliant appearance. Elegant equipages fill the streets, and the public promenades are crowded with throngs of pedestrians. A great amount of manufacturing is carried on in iron, steam-engines, screws, jewelry, and various articles of ornament and use. A visit to the different manufacturing establishments is full of curious interest. Connections may here be made by rail with Worcester, Hartford and Bristol, and by boat with Fall River and Newport. Various places of resort are to be found on either shore of Narragansett Bay.

In the early morning the train rushes through Pawtucket, a bustling village, the seat of Dunnell's famous Print Works; Attleborough, a place of extensive manufacturing in jewelry; Mansfield, where connection may be made with Taunton and New Bedford; Foxboro', Sharon, Canton, where a massive viaduct crosses the county road; West Roxbury, and Roxbury, to Boston, arriving at 5½ o'clock, A. M. A comfortable nap and a good breakfast may be enjoyed at the Winthrop, Adams, Marlboro', Tremont, Revere, Parker, or American House, before the cars start for the North.

It is needless in this connection, to speak of the numberless attractions of the city of BOSTON. Its splendid Common, its spacious State House, its well kept streets, its elegant and comfortable dwellings, its fine stores, its hospitable hotels, its large libraries, its cultivated society, are all too well known to demand a word of commendation. Its soil, too, is redolent of liberty. Griffin's Wharf, near which the Bostonians made their Tea with the harbor for a tea-pot; State street, the scene of the Boston Massacre; the great Tree on the Common, beneath whose branches the citizens met to concert their plans; Brattle St. Church, with a cannon ball imbedded in its side, are suggestive of the great struggle of the Revolution, whose first beginnings were made here. Bunker Hill Monument is but a mile distant; Cambridge, with Harvard University, the Washington Elm and Headquarters, and Mt. Auburn Cemetery, is half an hour's ride; Dorchester Heights still show the ruins of the old fortifications, which made the city untenable for the British troops, while Concord and Lexington are within visiting distance without great delay. The city of the Puritans, though a city of "notions," is still the chief city of New England and has well earned the title of the "Athens of America."

II. New York to Boston, via Newport and Fall River, on Long Island Sound by steamboat, from Fall River by rail, arriving at Boston at 5:30, A. M.

By this route you leave New York at the usual time by either of the fine steamers of the Fall River line—the Metropolis, or the Empire State. This line of travel extends through the whole length of Long Island Sound, and a part of Narraganset Bay. The distance is but ten or fifteen miles farther, the time and fare the same. The advantage of this route is that opportunity is afforded for a good night's rest on board the boat, and for the passage north from Boston without material detention. The disadvantage would be for passengers liable to sea-sickness that there is more open sea to be traversed, and Point Judith, with the "much-sounding" waves that beat upon it to be doubled. The boat arrives at Newport, an hour or two before dawn. This far-famed resort for pleasure-seekers requires no comment from us. The long-rolling surf and the white beeches, the ship-breaking rocks on the indented shore, the wide stretch of the Atlantic, are things not to be described. The dilletante and elegant may spend their days here in fashionable ennui, but the lover of nature will gratefully live in the midst of these enchanting scenes. The climate is soft and salubrious through the whole year. Excellent hotels open their hospitable doors. The facilities for sea-bathing are sufficiently numerous. The student of military science can visit Fort Adams, thought impregnable till the use of steam in war vessels has made fortifications of this kind useless. The antiquarian can puzzle his brains over the "Old Stone Mill," and be no wiser for his labors. The geologist will find a coal formation to explore and explain. The historical student may gratify his tastes by searching the traces of revolutionary conflicts, and the visits of the Northmen. Subjects of study and pleasure are in every direction.

BRISTOL is a maritime town engaged in considerable trade. FALL RIVER, where the cars are in waiting, is a manufacturing town, of some importance on Mount Hope Bay. Mount Hope is seen in the immediate neighborhood. Beyond, the route is through several villages, the most important of which are Middleboro',—junction with Cape Cod Railroad,—West Bridgewater,—junction with Plymouth Railroad,—Braintree, Quincy, and Dorchester. The cars arrive at Boston between 5 and 6 o'clock, A. M., in season to obtain breakfast and go North at 7:30, from the different depots.

III. NEW YORK TO BOSTON, via New London and Norwich; on Long Island Sound to Allyn's Point; thence by rail through Worcester, arriving at Boston about 5½, A. M.

The commodious Steamers COMMONWEALTH and CONNECTICUT leave their pier in New York at 5, P. M. These boats have few equals for elegance or comfort.

Starting from New York late in the afternoon, they make the passage through the East River into Long Island Sound before sunset. The other boats for Boston also start about the same time and pass over the same scenes. As they pass on the one side, the quiet suburbs of Brooklyn, Williamsburg and Green Point, and on the other the busy piers and streets of New York; the green islands, Blackwell's, Randall's, and others, which lie like emeralds upon the soft bosom of the river; the changing scenery, from urban bustle and activity, to rural stillness and solitude, the passenger on board will enjoy the calmness of the hour and the varied pleasure of the panoramic view. Soon the dangers of Hurlgate are passed, the sun sinks below the city, rapidly left behind, and the long reach of the Sound to the mouth of Thames River is to be sailed over in darkness. Half an hour after midnight, the landing at NEW LONDON is safely reached. A moment's stop to leave passengers and the course is continued up the river to ALLYN'S POINT. New London is a bustling city, engaged to a considerable extent in the whale fishery. The Arctic ship Resolute, abandoned by the English in Lancaster Sound, was encountered in Baffin's Bay by a New London whaler and safely brought into this port. The Griswold House, formerly a favorite resort for summer travellers, has just been destroyed by fire. Good accommodations are doubtless to be had. The PEQUOT HOUSE, a mile below, is well known. Fort Trumbull, near the Griswold House, needs nothing but a garrison to make it formidable to an enemy. At Allyn's Point, about 125 miles from New York, the passengers leave the steamers and take the cars for Worcester.

NORWICH is an active place, the seat of considerable trade, and a pleasant inland city. A number of small villages in Eastern Connecticut, and of manufacturing towns in Massachusetts, lie along the course of this railroad, being of no particular interest to the traveller. At four o'clock, A. M., the cars arrive at WORCESTER. If the tourist designs passing on to Concord, N. H., and thence up to the mountains, he will experience a detention of two hours and a half, which can well be passed in a comfortable nap, either at the LINCOLN, or the BAY STATE HOUSE. Both hotels are convenient to the depot, and unexceptionable, first class houses in every respect.

WORCESTER is the most enterprising city in New England, second only to Boston. It is well laid out, and its wide streets, lined with elegant private residences, stores and public buildings, invite the pedestrian to an early stroll. He will notice Horticultural Hall, Mechanics' Hall, a stately and imposing building, not surpassed in Massachusetts. The Female College occupies an elevated site in the southern part of the city. The College of the Holy Cross is still more distant. The Oread

Institute, a seminary of the highest order for young ladies, enjoys a deservedly wide reputation. The population of Worcester is over 20,000, and is rapidly increasing.

The cars, however, proceed directly on to Boston, arriving there at about the same time as by the other routes.

IV. New York to Boston, by railroad, via New Haven, Hartford, Springfield and Worcester.

The New York and Boston Express line—land route—is formed by the New York & New Haven, New Haven, Hartford & Springfield, Western and Boston & Worcester Railroads. The cars leave New York at 27th and 32nd streets at 8, A. M., and 3, P. M. The time to Boston is nine hours, and the fare $5.00. The cars proceed directly to Worcester Junction without change or detention. From Springfield to Worcester Junction, the Western Railroad passes through the thrifty, manufacturing and agricultural towns of central Massachusetts. Of these the principal are Palmer, Warren, West Brookfield, Brookfield and Spencer. The railroad stations on this road are the best in New England. To this remark, that at Worcester Junction is most decidedly an exception. The one storied, inconvenient, incommodious building at that point is a disgrace to the wealthy corporations, which, with unusual parsimony, have furnished this miserable shelter for the multitudes of passengers who are daily obliged to make it their temporary stopping place. The large travelling public demand better and worthier accommodations.

With slight detention, however, the cars proceed from Worcester, directly to Boston, where they arrive about 5 and 12 o'clock, P. M.

From Boston to the mountains there are, as before indicated, three distinct routes.

I. BOSTON TO GORHAM, N. H., VIA PORTLAND.

It is only a few years that the valleys of the Eastern and Northern slopes of the Mountains have been open to travellers. Until the Atlantic & St. Lawrence Railroad, which connects Portland and Montreal, was completed through Northern New-Hampshire, some seven years ago, they were inaccessible to the tourists for pleasure, and their charms were unsuspected.

The forms of the mountains are bolder, and the slopes more abrupt, on the Eastern and Northern sides. There is more beauty around North Conway and in the Pemigewasset valley; but the most satisfactory impressions of mountain ruggedness, strength, and sublimity are gained from the views that surround GORHAM, N. H., and "The GLEN."

One can reach the great White Mountain range from Boston more speedily and with more ease by the Portland route than by any other. The traveller leaves Boston for Portland in the morning, by either the Eastern Railroad, or the Boston & Maine. He reaches Portland at noon, and has half an hour for dinner in the ample and commodious Station House of the Atlantic & St. Lawrence, or "Grand Trunk," Railway. At 1 o'clock he takes the cars on this road, and at 5, P. M., is landed in front of the ALPINE HOUSE, in Gorham, N. H. This Hotel is one of the largest and best in the whole mountain region, and has been for some years under the charge of Mr. JOHN R. HITCHCOCK. There is ample time in the long summer days for a stroll or a ride, from this Hotel after supper, along the banks of the noble Androscoggin river and in full view of the highest summits of the White Hills and the great Mount Moriah range. Or if the traveller's time is very limited, he can take a stage from the door of the ALPINE HOUSE, on the arrival of the cars at five o'clock, and in two hours can reach the "GLEN HOUSE," eight miles distant,—a spacious, excellent and well known Hotel at the base of Mount Washington, under the charge of Mr. J. M. THOMPSON.

Thus, by this Portland route, one can reach Gorham and its charming scenery in ten hours from Boston, with time for dinner and rest; or can arrive at the very base of Mount Washington in twelve hours. The cars of the Grand Trunk Railway from Portland to the Mountains are of the most commodious kind. The road is the wide, or five feet and a half gauge. It is very rarely that the trains fail to keep time like a chronometer; and the conductors are celebrated for their gentlemanly readiness to impart full information to passengers concerning the mountain routes and scenery.

There is, also, communication by steamboat between Boston and Portland. Leaving Boston about seven in the evening, Portland is reached at five in the morning. Then by the first train on the Grand Trunk Railway, the traveller arrives at Gorham at 11, A. M., and at the Glen House, if he desires, by stage in season for dinner. The fare from Boston to Gorham by a through ticket on the cars is $4; by steamboat and cars, $3.00. The distance from Boston to Portland by the shorter of the two railroad routes is 106 miles; from Portland to Gorham, N. H., 91 miles.

On the route from Portland to Gorham, there is nothing especially attractive in the scenery,—nothing that promises or hints the grandeur in reserve, until the train reaches

Bryant's Pond. This lake in miniature, the source of the Little Androscoggin river, charmingly set among hills several hundred feet in height, is twenty-nine miles from Gorham. The pond and the track of the railroad lie about seven hundred feet above the sea level.

The next point of interest is Bethel, the chief town of Oxford County, Maine, and probably the loveliest village of that State. It is twenty-one miles from Gorham. Travellers are as yet but little acquainted with its attractions. Bethel is, in truth, the North Conway of the Eastern side of the Hills. If the terminus of the Railroad were here, or if passengers were

9

compelled to leave the cars at this point, and take stages to Gorham and the Glen, Bethel would be a dangerous rival to North Conway, and the ride from Bethel to Mount Washington would be pronounced superior, on some accounts, in charm to the famous ride from Conway through Bartlett to the Notch.

The meadows of Bethel are very lovely; and on a clear afternoon, when the golden light falls aslant upon the fresh grass, throwing out long shadows from the trees, and the eye follows northward the narrowing line of hills along the course of the Androscoggin, and catches the sharp edges of the great White Mountain range sweeping across and closing up the vista, it is difficult to conceive where an artist can find a more tempting picture in New-England. There are several hills, too, in and near the village, easily accessible, around which the most fascinating panoramas of forests, hills, rivers, lakes, meadows, and mountain majesty are displayed. Bethel will, we predict, at some time not very far distant, be sought as a boarding-place during the summer by those who love charming scenery with more quiet than the prominent White Mountain routes and hotels afford.

There is a comfortable hotel in Bethel, kept by Mr. CHANDLER. Travellers can procure teams from him to visit places of interest in the neighborhood. There is a delightful drive of twelve miles to the grand water-sculpture of the Albany Basins. Eighteen miles in the opposite direction one finds the Rumford Falls. The road to these Falls is excellent, the scenery on the way very lovely, and the Falls themselves are hardly inferior to any in New-England. The full tide of the Androscoggin makes a descent here of one hundred and sixty feet, in three pitches, and within the space of a quarter of a mile. There is a fine excursion also from Bethel to the Speckled Mountain Notch, or Bear River Notch, as it is sometimes called. The farther end of this Notch is about eighteen miles from Bethel. The road for twelve miles—part of the way up the valley of

View of Bethel, Me.

the Bear River—is excellent, and very good accommodation is found there at the "POPLAR TAVERN."

The "Screw-Auger Fall," at Fanning's Mills, and the ride up through the jaws of the Notch will well repay the time which the journey requires. Starting early in the morning from Bethel, the excursion and return can easily be made in a day. Or it will be practicable to push through from the Bear River Notch to Umbagog Lake in another day, and thence to Dixville Notch, of which we shall speak bye and bye. The trout fishing on this route is probably unsurpassed in New England.

From Bethel to the Station in Gorham, the scenery through which the cars pass is very fascinating. Three villages, charmingly located to increase the beauty of the landscape, lie in full view from the train,—West Bethel, Gilead, and Shelburne. About a mile from the Station in Gilead, the boundary line of Maine is passed, and the traveller is among the New Hampshire hills. Especially fortunate are those who see this scenery for the first time in the rich light of a clear summer afternoon. The sight of the brilliant meadows spotted with elms; of the graceful curves of the Androscoggin, studded with islands; of the brawny hills that guard it, among which the train flies along a twisted track; and, now and then, of the long, firmly cut lines of the White Mountain ridge shooting across the north, until in Shelburne, Madison, and the peak of Jefferson, and the bulk of Washington spring out for a few minutes in full view, almost banishes the fatigue of a hot day's ride, and prepares the visitor for the pleasures in store after his arrival in Gorham, at the Alpine House.

The route through the mountain region from this point is described on the 5th and following pages.

But we must here speak of two excursions to other points of interest connected directly with the White Mountains on their eastern side. The first is to

LANCASTER, N. H.

This is the shire town of Cöos County, and is set amid some

of the noblest and loveliest scenery of New England. The whole range of the White Mountains, the great Franconia hills, and many of the Green Mountains are in full view from some of its streets. Then, too, the Connecticut meadows are among the finest here which the river can boast in its whole extent. The drives in the neighborhood, on either side the Connecticut, are unsurpassed, probably, in New England; for the roads are excellent, and the views are very various. And a spacious Hotel has just been completed there, which will afford attractive accommodation to travellers. There are few points among, or near, the mountains, where so much quiet pleasure could be experienced in a visit of a few weeks, as in Lancaster.

There is a stage from Gorham to Lancaster, passing through the grand scenery of Jefferson. The distance is 24 miles. One can also take the train in the forenoon, or afternoon, from Gorham, reach Northumberland in an hour, take a stage thence to Lancaster, some ten miles distant.

We must also call attention to the scenery of the

Dixville Notch.

The Dixville hills lie in the extreme northern portion of New Hampshire, some sixty miles beyond the Washington range. It is very seldom that a tourist strays so far from the regular routes; but the geologists have long been acquainted with the interesting scenery of the region, and have called attention to it in reports of their surveys. Dr. Jackson, in his great work on the Geology of New Hampshire, speaks of the Dixville Notch as more Alpine in its character than any other pass of our New England mountains, and predicts that its grandeur will yet make it a place of large resort.

Since the completion of the Atlantic and St. Lawrence Railroad, it has become easily accessible and should be more widely known. One can leave Boston at 7 o'clock in the morning, and sleep the same night within 10 miles of it, reaching it early in the forenoon of the second day. Or travellers can take the cars at 11 from the Alpine House in Gorham, and in an hour and a half be landed at North Stratford, which lies on the Connecticut River, thirty-six miles from Gorham. The Railroad ride is very pleasant. The track lies along the narrow and winding valley of the Androscoggin, hemmed in by grand and gloomy hills, until it bends toward the more cheerful Connecticut. Then it winds up around the base of the singular, bleached, twin cones, called the Stratford Peaks.

At North Stratford a wagon stage is in readiness, on the arrival of the noon and evening trains, to convey passengers to Colebrook. If there is no stage, an extra wagon can easily be hired. The ride to Colebrook up the Connecticut, is really charming. Frequently a view of a broad intervale, with the glittering river sweeping through it in a lordly curve, will make a man regret that the slow pace of the horses could not be retarded, in order that he might more leisurely feast his eyes.

Colebrook is quite a flourishing village on the New Hampshire side of the river, and lying in the eastern shadow of a massive and majestic mountain which the inhabitants call Monadnoc. This hill lies just beyond the river in Vermont, and is really quite imposing by its bulk and glorious verdure. It must spring more than two thousand feet from the stream at its base. One arrives in Colebrook usually about four in the afternoon. Dixville Notch is only ten miles distant. But there is no public house near it, and it is best to pass the night at the inn kept, we believe, by Mr. Cummings in Colebrook, and called the Monadnoc House. If a person before going there will look at the situation of the village on the map, and observe that it is within almost a stone's throw of Canada, he will doubtless be most pleasantly disappointed with the substantial accommodations furnished by the brisk and obliging landlord. One had better leave the hotel about seven the next morning for the Notch and give the whole day to the excursion. The road is very good, but rises steadily the whole distance ; so that the ten miles demands three hours' riding. Travellers will be much struck with the general excellence of the land along the way. It is the best farming region of the Granite State ; and the fields are so free from stones, that it is really impossible to have stone walls for boundaries. The last two miles of the ride wind through the grandest forest one will find in his mountain travels. Every variety of tree is represented along the way, and generally of much larger growths than are met before. A person will begin to doubt whether there is any mountain magnificence near, so closely is the road shut in by the forest. Suddenly the heavy walls of the Dixville range begin to show themselves ahead. And while one is admiring their dark and grave sides of shadowed foliage, wondering where the pass he is in search of can open, a turn of the road to the right brings the wagon in front of the bare and savage jaws of the Notch, at its western entrance.

The first view of it is very impressive. It opens like a Titanic gateway to some region of vast and mysterious desolation. The pass is much narrower than either of the more famed ones in the White Mountains, and through its whole extent of a mile and a quarter, has more the character of a Notch. One cannot but feel that the mountain was rent apart by some volcanic convulsion, and the two sides left to tell the story by their correspondence and the naked dreariness of the pillars of rotting rock that face each other. There is little more than room for a road at the bottom; and the walls slope away from it so sharply that considerable outlay is required from the State, every year, to clear it of the stones and earth which the frosts and rain roll into it every winter and spring.

No description can impart an adequate conception of the mournful grandeur of the decaying cliffs of mica slate which overhang the way. They shoot up in most singular and fantastic shapes, and vary in height from four hundred to eight hundred feet. A few centuries ago, the pass must have been very wild, but the pinnacles of rock which give the scenery such an Alpine character, are rapidly crumbling away. Some have decayed to half their original height. And the side walls of the Notch are strewn with *debris* which the ice and storms have pried and gnawed from the decrepit cliffs. The whole aspect is one of ruin and wreck. The creative forces seem to have retreated from the spot, and abandoned it to the sport of the destructive elements. One might entertain the thought that some awful crime had been committed there, for which the region was blasted by a lasting curse. The only life in the Notch belongs to the raspberry vines. It seems to be the paradise of this delicious fruit.

One should climb the highest pinnacle which juts out from the southerly wall of the pass, and stands about eight hundred feet above the road. It is no easy task to keep the footing in the steep ascent over the loose and treacherous ruins of slate that strew the way. Hands and feet are necessary. We once knew a company of gentlemen who would have been discouraged once or twice, were it not that the lady of the party proved so sure footed and steady a climber, and laughed at difficulties.

She belongs to Boston and is a model traveller. It will be found, however, that the view from the summit repays the toil of the scramble. It is no small trial for weak nerves to walk out upon the side of the Notch upon this cliff, not more than six feet wide and eight hundred feet sheer down. No part of the ride up Mount Washington makes the head swim so giddily. From it one can easily see into Maine, Vermont, and Canada. Only a few miles east, lies Lake Umbagog, where the moose congregate in the evening to stand up to their neck in water and "fight flies," as the guides express it. About ten miles north is Lake Connecticut, a beautiful sheet of water, mother of the noble river which is the pride of New England. One might spend a few days very profitably in exploring the novelties of the districts that lie around the Notch.

After about an hour's stay upon the pinnacle, one should descend and ride through the pass to a flume just beyond its eastern gateway. A more interesting ride can hardly be found in the whole White Moutain region. The Notch is crescent in its shape, which adds to the effect of height, by concealing the whole extent at a single glance. Everywhere, as you ride through, are these sad and sullen cliffs, the monuments of a majesty fast passing away.

How charming, then, the surprise, in passing through the Notch eastward, to ride out from its spiky teeth of slate into a most lovely plain, called "The Clear Stream Meadows," embosomed in mountains luxuriantly wooded to the crown. It is something like descending from the desolation of the Alps into the foliage and beauty of Italy. There is but one house near. But the graves of the earliest settler and his wife are there, fenced off rudely, and overgrown with the tall weeds which nature wears for them. How many of the great and wealthy of our land will find such a cemetery? A mountain range for a monument; a luxuriant valley for a grave; such silence to sleep in as no Mount Auburn can assure, and their story told to visitants from far off portions of the land!

Returning through the whole length of the Notch, Colebrook is reached again by supper-time. The next morning, one can take the stage-wagon to North Stratford, and thence reach Gorham by cars early in the forenoon. Thus the whole journey from the Alpine House, or Glen House, to Dixville Notch, and back again, can be made in two days; and nearly the whole of one day will be passed in the Notch. It is also one of the cheapest excursions which the mountain region affords.

WILLOUGHBY LAKE,

should also be mentioned. This is a small sheet of water, six miles in length, and from one to two in width, charmingly set between steep granite mountains in the Northern part of Vermont. There is a fine hotel on the border of the lake kept by ALONZO BEMIS. Passengers can leave Gorham about noon by cars, stop at the ISLAND POND HOUSE for dinner and take the stage thence for Willoughby Lake, which will be reached by tea time. A few days can be most delightfully passed there. More will be said of this lake in another connection.

ISLAND POND is the "half-way" station between Portland and Montreal. It is a charming spot. The pond is directly in front of the Station House. In high water, the Clyde, the regular outlet, pours its water into Memphremagog, and thence into the St. Lawrence, while an outlet at the other end leads into the Connecticut and thence into Long Island Sound. To trace up the Clyde by a canoe would make a pleasant excursion. Mr. WHITEHOUSE, the accommodating landlord of the hotel, will furnish all the necessary accommodations. The fishing all around is excellent.

PORTLAND, ME., TO CONWAY, N. H.

Distance to Conway, 58 miles. Fare, $2.50. The route to Conway, via Portland and Gorham, Me., was very attractive and much patronized before the Atlantic & St. Lawrence Railroad was opened to Gorham, N. H. Since then the steamboat which runs over Sebago Lake has been withdrawn for want of patronage and the route has fallen into comparative disuse. Persons, however, wishing to spend time upon the journey will find this a very pleasant ride.

The tourist leaves Portland by the cars of the Portland & Kennebeck Railroad at 7:15, A. M. A ride of half an hour brings you to Gorham, Me., ten miles distant, where you take the coach for Conway. At Livingston (seventeen miles from Gorham,) you cross the Saco, and thence winding along its banks for eleven miles the

GREAT FALLS are reached. These constitute one of the great attractions of the route and are said to be "unsurpassed in grandeur and sublimity." Twelve miles farther on we reach

FRYEBURG, the seat of a flourishing Academy. Here are situated "LOVELL'S POND," famed for an Indian battle, and Jockey Cap, Stark's, and Pine Hills. A ride of eight miles farther brings us to Conway about 7 o'clock, P. M. The stage leaves Conway for Portland, daily, early in the morning.

Fine distant views of the mountains are gained all along the route. Conway and the route thence to the Notch will be spoken of hereafter.

II. BOSTON TO WHITE MOUNTAIN NOTCH, VIA DOVER, ALTON BAY, CENTRE HARBOR AND CONWAY.

Distance from Boston to Alton Bay, 96 miles.

The cars leave the station house of the Boston & Maine Railroad every morning at 7:30. At Dover, connection is made with the Cochecho Railroad for Alton Bay. This was originally christened "Merrymeeting Bay." The hotel, depot, and steamboat wharf constitute almost the only buildings at this place. Various Indian relics have been found near here, and are in the possession of Capt. SANBORN. Mr. COFFIN, the landlord of the Hotel, has at all times every convenience for riding and fishing.

The Steamer DOVER, a new and elegant Lake steamer, has been enlarged during the past winter, and is now 132 feet in length, and moves with great rapidity and steadiness. From Alton Bay the steamer will convey you to Wolfborough, ten miles, and thence to Centre Harbor, twenty miles farther. A good dinner may be obtained on board the boat, or at the Senter House. The Boat reaches Centre Harbor about 1, P. M. From Centre Harbor you can proceed directly to Conway, as will be described hereafter. The advantage of this route is the additional distance passed on Lake Winnipisaukee.

The Lake and the route from Centre Harbor will be spoken of hereafter.

III. BOSTON TO WHITE MOUNTAINS *via* CONCORD, N. H.

The traveller leaves Boston for Concord, either by the cars of the Boston & Maine Railroad, from Haymarket Square, or of the Lowell Railroad, from Causeway street. Should he take the former route, he will pass through Somerville, Malden, and Melrose, all pretty villages in the suburbs of Boston; South Reading, where connections may be made with Salem and Newburyport; Reading and Wilmington, of no particular note; Wilmington Junction, where the track crosses the Salem and Lowell Railroad; Andover, the seat of Phillips' Academy, and the celebrated Theological Seminary, of the Trinitarian Congregationalists.

LAWRENCE. This is a manufacturing city, recently built on the Merrimack river, ten miles below Lowell, and similar in character to that place. It contains manufactories of cotton and woolen goods, shawls, duck, iron, &c. It is a promising place. Here the Manchester & Lawrence Railroad diverges from the Boston & Maine, and passes on through Methuen, Salem, N. H., Windham, Derry, and Londonderry, to Manchester, where a union is effected with the train on the Concord Railroad from below.

On leaving Boston by the Boston & Lowell Railroad, the traveller will pass through SOMERVILLE, WEST MEDFORD, WINCHESTER, WOBURN—suburban villages, much sought for by business men for a quiet, rural residence — WILMINGTON, and BILLERICA to

LOWELL. This is a place famous through the whole country for its extensive manufactures. It is built near Pawtucket Falls, upon the Merrimack. A wide canal, whose massive masonry is a remarkable instance of the power of persevering industry, conveys the necessary water to the wheels, that carry the machinery of the mills. Carpets, cotton and woolen goods, prints, and other similar articles are manufactured, employing a capital of $11,000,000 in public corporations, and 13,000 laborers, besides the large number engaged in private enterprise. Lowell is a brisk city, and has enjoyed a great degree of prosperity.

NASHUA is a thriving, bustling manufacturing town at the confluence of the Nashua and Merrimack rivers. It presents no objects of particular interest. The Pearl Street, Central, and Indian Head Houses are old hotels of established character.

REED'S FERRY, or MERRIMACK, is the site of a fine academy, which stands near the railroad track, on a high bluff overlooking a wide expanse of country. GOFF'S FALLS are in the town of Bedford, and are to be seen from the car window. Here the road crosses the Merrimack, and the train soon arrives at

MANCHESTER, a very enterprising city, almost wholly devoted to manufacturing. Here the Manchester & Lawrence Railroad intersects. Both corporations, now united under one management, are profitably and energetically conducted by J. A. GILMORE, who, in all matters of business, is a host in himself. Opposite Manchester may be noticed Point Raymond, and the Unconoonucs, two round hills in the interior. Manchester is well planned, and is evidently determined to distance all competitors in the State, in enterprise and vigorous growth. The AMOSKEAG FALLS are a mile above the city, and furnish a fine water privilege. A short distance farther, on the right, may be seen the new Reform School, quite an imposing edifice of brick.

MARTIN'S FERRY is a station to accommodate some village not visible from the cars. At HOOKSETT, the cars again cross the river. On the left may be observed a high, conical hill, called the Pinnacle, rising abruptly from the plain. From its summit may be seen an extensive and charming prospect. On the right are the Hooksett Falls, a pleasant object, as the white foam appears amid the rapidly descending waters. Eight miles farther is

CONCORD,

the capital of New Hampshire. This may afford interest sufficient to detain the traveller for a short time, while he examines the large and well conducted Prison of solid granite; or the State House of similar material, chaste in its design and perfect in its finish; or the Asylum for the Insane, with beautiful grounds and a commanding site. A fine view of the city may be obtained from the cupola of the State House. Around the town are pleasant drives skirting the shores of Pennacook Lake or Long Pond, Turkey Pond and the river. A beautiful prospect may be obtained near sunset from Point Pleasant on the high bluffs of the Merrimack. Not far from the village on the road to St. Paul's School, is erected a monument to the memory of some of the early martyrs to the "bloudy salvages" who infested the region. Elsewhere is pointed out the location of an old fort; and buildings, still tenanted, bear the marks of both ball and bullet. The Methodist Biblical Institute is in the building known as the Old North Church, for a long time the only church in the town. A visit to the numerous cotton factories, as well as to the large flouring mill recently erected at Fisherville, may serve as an agreeable terminus to an hour's ride.

There are three fine and commodious Hotels in Concord:— The Phenix, by CORNING & CLARK, the Eagle by DUMAS & NORTON, and the American by JOHN GASS. These are not anywhere excelled for the accommodations they afford the traveller or the conveniences they place around him.

The amount of railroad building, work, furniture, etc., here visible, is probably superior to any in places of even twice its size, throughout the country. It is the Depôt of five distinct railways, and, at the hours of half-past ten and three, when the great trains, northward and southward, are made up, a scene of apparently irremedible confusion is presented to the spectator, not unfrequently adorned with quite novel and amusing incidents. The Coach Manufactories of the Messrs. Abbots' and the Messrs. Downings' are not far from the Depot, and are worthy of visit. The last train from Boston remains here over night, and thus is afforded the tourist his last opportunity for obtaining any articles he may be in need of during his journey.

From Concord, four distinct routes to the mountain region, present themselves to the traveller. One is over the Northern, and the other three over the Montreal Railroad.

1. CONCORD TO FRANCONIA, via Northern, Connecticut & Passumpsic, and White Mountains Railroad. Distance 140 miles; from Boston, 212. Fare from Boston to Franconia, $8.00. From Concord, $5.50. Time from Boston, 12 hours.

The Northern Railroad extends from Concord to White River Junction, following the course of the Merrimack as far as Franklin, when it crosses to the Connecticut over the high lands of central New Hampshire. The road is admirably conducted, and furnishes a favorite route. At Fisherville, the road crosses the Contoocook River, and Dustin's Island, so named from its being the camping ground of a party of Indians, from whom a captive woman, Mrs. Dustin, made her escape in colonial times. Just before reaching Franklin, the traveller will notice upon the right of the track, the former residence of the late Hon. Daniel Webster. It is a comfortable, old fashioned house, among the trees, and just the place to furnish repose to the statesman, jaded in the conflicts of party and of the forum. Franklin is a busy village. At Potter Place, may be seen on the left of the track, Mt. Kearsarge, in Salisbury and Wilmot, two thousand four hundred and sixty-one feet high; on the right, the Ragged Mountains, rough and unshapely. Danbury will furnish a capital dinner to those accustomed to masticate rapidly. Cardigan mountain may be seen from Grafton. At Enfield is a beautiful pond, on whose shores a community of Shakers have a neat settlement. Through Lebanon and East Lebanon, the train passes to

White River Junction, where the road crosses the Connecticut, and a union is effected with the trains from the valley of the Connecticut. This place is important only from the fact, that it is the convergent and divergent point of the eight railroad trains, which here meet and separate over the Passumpsic, Northern, and Vermont Central Railroads. It is distant from New York, 265 miles; from Boston 152 via Fitchburg, 142 via Lowell; from Wells River 40; from Willoughby Lake 80; and from Franconia Notch 60 miles. Considerable self-possession and self-control are requisite at this point, on the part of the traveller, lest he lose his baggage, his seat, his temper, and, most of all, his way. If he becomes flurried, he is in great danger of taking the "back track" for Concord, or of going against his will to Burlington, Vt., or of flying wildly to Bellows Falls, Vt. In the calmest state of mind, let him—after refreshment, for which there is ample time,—step into the cars of the *Passumpsic* Railroad, sure that he is right, and he will soon go ahead through, perhaps, the most delightful region of country, which he has yet seen.

The Connecticut & Passumpsic Rivers Railroad at present connects White River and Barton. It is designed to extend it to Canada. The road is in the valley of the Connecticut until it reaches Barnet; from thence it is over and along the Passumpsic.

The extent and variety of the scenery on this portion of the route is greater than is ever imagined by those who have never visited it. The great diversity and contrast of the views are alone sufficient to astonish and delight. Hill and valley, precipice and plain—sharp angular declivities, without a vestige of verdure, and smooth smiling meadow lands covered with the greenest sward and the heaviest crops,—a great surface of river on the one hand, unruffled and seemingly motionless, a little mountain stream on the other, dashed into foam by the speed of its descent—all these totally different and dissimilar prospects are so intermingled with one another, as to be a constant source of surprise and satisfaction.

But divested of these more distant views there is still something startling in the sudden changes presented to the eye over the very track itself; at one instant the cars are sweeping smoothly along the most beautiful of meadows—the next they are, apparently, penned within the solid rock, that rises fifty feet upon either hand; they dash out upon a great embankment, that is invisible, and seemingly fly across the chasm which is beneath—they tremble along the lofty grade which falls precipitously into the darkness and resonance of a bridge—emerge to sunlight by the side of some beautiful pond, and slowly draw to a halt in a quiet New England village.

Norwich and Hanover, 4 miles on, are out of sight. Norwich is the seat of a military University. Hanover, on the New Hampshire side, is the location of Dartmouth College.

Ompompanoosuc is 9 miles farther on. It receives its name from an Indian stream near by which signifies, "The very clear rocky river of the hills." A copperas mine is near by.

North Thetford is 7½ miles distant. Between this station and the next there is a very good view of several mountains on the New Hampshire side. Mt. Cuba is the highest of these peaks, and is said to contain a scanty population of bears—which from its barren appearance may well be credited. A conical peak, to the right of Mt. Cuba is termed Sunday

Mountain. It looms up blue and melancholy in the distance, its summit destitute of vegetation and its sides scarred by avalanches. Black Mountain and Mt. Sago are beyond.

On leaving FAIRLEE, the Moosehillock Mountain, four thousand eight hundred and seven feet high,

"Upheaves its huge bare back emergent,"

and for nearly twenty miles remains in sight.

NEWBURY, 35 miles from White River, is chiefly noted for its SULPHUR SPRINGS, as infallible a specific as Patent Medicine for many diseases. Passing through a tremendous cut in the solid rock, we reach

WELLS RIVER, the junction of the Montreal, the Passumpsic, and the White Mountains Railroads. The latter is the road necessary for reaching Franconia. There is no detention, and the cars are soon making their way up the Ammonoosuc River. The opening of this road, while it has accommodated the host of travellers in this direction, has materially diminished the patronage of two excellent hotels, the Wells River House, and the Coosack House, where, if desired, a comfortable home may be found for any one wishing for a quiet summer retreat. At the former house, was to be seen a year or two since, a stable of the finest Morgan horses in the country—young, sound, unblemished, fast, and beautifully symmetrical.

BATH is distant five miles from Wells River, and is a very neat and prosperous place. A good hotel—the BATH—may be found here, and there is fine fishing, as well as fine scenery in the neighborhood.

LISBON in a quiet village, in no way remarkable except for the indications which are here clearly given of an approach to the highlands. The mountains are seen in the distance, and, on a fine summer afternoon, the effect of the landscape is very exhilarating.

LITTLETON is the terminus of railroad travel in this direction, and is reached about 5 o'clock, P. M. Stages are in readiness to start immediately for the Franconia Notch and the White Mountain Notch, the former distant twelve, the latter eighteen miles, with fares at one and two dollars respectively.

Having taken on board the evening mail for the denizens of the mountain region, and waited long enough for the passengers to snatch a hasty meal at the Union, or the White Mountain House, the stage coaches are off upon their course for the long desired goal. For twelve miles, the road winds along in the valleys and ascends the hills, through the little villages of Bethlehem and Franconia. The land rises on either side, its highest elevations softly burnished by the setting sun. The mountains in the distance glow with a more radiant light. Gradually, the shadows steal up their sides, as the sun goes down. Darkness settles in the valley. The passengers beguile the way with "Stage Coach Stories," or gaze in an admiring silence on the varied landscape, as the "last rays of departing day linger and play upon the summits" of the neighboring hills. An occasional cabin is now only to be seen along the road-side. Soon, even this slight symptom of human life disappears. In the deepening shades of evening, the coach rattles, for two or three miles, through a gloomy piece of dark forest, and by nine o'clock, the careful driver has brought his precious freight safely to the door of the hotel. The bright lights, the cosy fire in the open chimney, the sounds of merry voices, and the cordial greetings of friends, welcome the arriving party to the abundant cheer, and the generous hospitality of the Profile House.

2. Concord to White Mountains, via Montreal Railroad.

Three different routes are presented to the tourist over this road. (1.) He may go to Wells River, thence over the White Mountains Railroad to Littleton and down to Franconia by stage as by the Northern Railroad just described. (2) He may leave the cars at Plymouth and proceed directly to the Flume House by stage. (3) The cars may be left at the

Weirs, and the traveller may pursue his journey to the White Mountain Notch, via Centre Harbor and Conway.

1. Cars to Littleton. This route is shorter than by the Northern Railroad, though passengers arrive at the Profile, or White Mountain House at the same time as by the other route. It has the advantage of skirting along the shores of Lake Winnipisaukee. The change of cars and confusion of White River Junction is also avoided. The distance is 124 miles; from Boston, 198. Fare from Boston to Franconia, $7.50. Time from Boston, twelve hours.

Should the preference be given for the route over the Montreal Railroad, the tourist will find the cars of the road ready to start upon the arrival of the train from Boston. The road crosses the Merrimack River, soon after leaving the Concord station, and continues up that river upon its eastern bank, through the villages of Canterbury, Northfield, Sanbornton Bridge,—where the road crosses a portion of Lake Winnipisaukee, called the Great Bay—Laconia, and Lake Village to "Weirs." Here the Steamer Lady of the Lake, Capt. Wm. Walker, Jr., is ready to start for Centre Harbor. As a description of this Lake will be given hereafter, we will not detain the reader at this point.

Laconia is the stopping place for Gilford, where the traveller will find a good hotel kept by A. L. Morrison. Mt. Belknap, four and a half miles distant is much visited. The Canterbury Shakers are only twelve miles distant — a pleasant ride. The citizens are very hospitable. The Lake, also, may be visited from this place.

We pass rapidly through Meredith Village and Holderness, and arrive at Plymouth soon after noon. Having fortified the inner man with the good cheer of our jolly host, Burnham, we return to the cars, and proceeding through Quincy, Rumney, Wentworth, Warren and Haverhill, with Carr's mountain, Mooschillock, and the spurs of the Franconia range in sight, reach Wells River. Here a junction is made with the cars from below on the Passumpsic route, and the White Mountains Road, and the train after a short detention goes on to Littleton. (See page 114.)

MOOSEHILLOCK MOUNTAIN, as has just been said, is in sight from the road between Plymouth and Wells River. As this mountain is one of the highest in the vicinity, some tourists may desire to visit it. To do this, they should leave the cars at Warren, twenty miles from Plymouth. Two small hotels, the UNION and the GRAFTON HOUSE, here provide for the accommodation of guests. Three or four miles from the village is a lead mine. The company commenced operations only last year. The five miles to the base of Moosehillock can easily be passed over in a carriage. A bridle-path was constructed to its summit during the past season and a large company from Concord, N. H., made the ascent in September. Prof. A. Guyot, also made an excursion to this mountain, and, we are permitted to make the following extract from a letter written by him, descriptive of the view:

"The panorama which is before your eyes at the summit of Moosehillock is nearly the most extensive I have found in New England, not excepting even that from Mts. Washington and Lafayette, over which it possesses many advantages. This is due to the insulated position of that mountain outside of the group of the White Mountains proper, combined with its great elevation, which surpasses by 1,000 feet to 1,500 feet the surrounding heights, while it is less than 500 below the summit of Lafayette. The eye thus embraces at a single glance in the north and northeast all the chains of the White Mountain group from Lafayette and Mt. Washington to the high peaks of the central, southern and eastern chains in Sandwich and Conway. Towards the northwest the view extends into Canada; on the west and southwest the whole State of Vermont with its long and continuous chain of the Green Mountains; towards the south and east the whole State of New Hampshire, with its innumerable scattered hills and lakes, among which Winnipisaukee is conspicuous, and a part of Maine, complete the grand, instructive, raised map which is opened before the beholder. Moosehillock, which is now so accessible by the way of the Boston, Concord & Montreal Railroad, and by means of a path, recently cut through the forest to the summit, deserves to take a distinguished place among the high summits visited by the lovers of mountain scenery."

It is in contemplation to construct a road from Warren to Franconia. If this is done, it will be the shortest route to Franconia, the distance being only fourteen miles. From the summit of Moosehillock to Franconia the distance is only eight miles.

Those who desire to visit Lakes Willoughby and Memphremagog will continue their journey from Wells River over the Connecticut and Passumpsic Railroad to St. Johnsbury, Barton, and Derby. At Barton stages leave for Lake Willoughby upon the arrival of the cars from below. The distance is but seven miles over a good road.

Derby is on the south-eastern shore of Lake Memphremagog, and is a pleasant town on the verge of the State of Vermont. These two places must not be omitted from the programme of pleasure travel. They abound in the finest scenery of all this region, and can be reached with comparative ease and at a moderate expense. A number of small streams run into Lake Memphremagog from the south, and numerous ponds, well stocked with different varieties of fish, are to be found in all this section, agreeably diversifying the face of the country. The hills upon the shores lie pleasantly basking in the sunshine, and the whole place ever breathes the sweet influence of contentment and peace. Those who know the region, and the route thither need not be reminded of its quiet and repose, while those who have yet the pleasure in reserve need but a single suggestion, to induce them to include a visit to the locality in the plan of their summer tour.

WILLOUGHBY LAKE

is a beautiful sheet of water, between six and seven miles in length, and varying from half a mile to two miles in width. It is of a crescent shape, with little inlets and promontories along its shores. It is within a gap or chasm of the Green Mountain range, and forms a great reservoir for the brooks in the immediate vicinity. The waters of the Lake discharge, through a small stream, into the St. Francis and thence into the St. Lawrence. The brooks and rivulets, however, which are crossed a few rods before reaching the Hotel, flow into the Passumpsic and down the Connecticut.

The loveliness of the Lake is greatly enhanced by the rough and precipitous scenery around it. The Lake is all beauty and repose, while the mountains, that rise abruptly from its shores, are rough and angular.

At some remote day, the two peaks, that now tower on either side of the Lake, undoubtedly formed a single summit, and were separated by some of the volcanic throes whose traces are so visible throughout this region. Mt. Ananance, the peak upon the eastern shore, is one thousand nine hundred and fifty feet high. It receives its name from a chief of the St. Francis tribe which once lived here. A modern attempt to christen it "Pisgah" has fortunately been unsuccessful. The unnamed summit confronting Mt. Ananance, on the opposite side of the Lake, is fifteen hundred feet high. Here, a short distance from the water, there is a sparse growth of pine, fir, spruce, cedar and hemlock, rapidly dwindling into dwarf birch and shrubs. The soil they cover is thin and rocky, evidently a *detritus* from the mountains. This vegetation is on an angle, from the side of the mountain, of at least forty-five degrees, and extends up about six hundred feet. It is terminated by the solid rock which rises, from above the tree tops, a thousand feet perpendicularly. A forest of stunted pine and hemlock bristles around the summit, cleared away, however, for a little space on the highest elevation, so as to afford a view of the surrounding country.

From this observatory, easily attained on horseback and nearly reached with a carriage, there is a most beautiful landscape visible. Lake Memphremagog and Owl's Head Mountain are twenty miles to the north; Lake Champlain and its shipping fifty miles to the westward; every prominent part of the White Mountains, the entire range of the Green Mountains, Massaweepee Lake, — the beautiful pond in Westmoreland, Burke and Newark — are all fairly visible from the summit of Mt. Ananance.

Near the "Devil's Den," — a doubtful looking hole in the rock, about midway down the Lake shore, — it is said no soundings can be obtained, although fabulous quantities of line have been expended in the attempt. Above this spot, some six hundred feet on the hill side, and just at the base of a precipitous rock, there is, what has been named, the Flower Garden — a spot where all varieties of wild plants grow and blossom. And still higher than the Flower Garden, in the rock itself, where the foot of man never trod and probably never will, is the Eagle's Eyrie. All these spots, and the traces of many an avalanche and land slide, may be seen by the tourist in sailing down the Lake.

The Willoughby Lake House, by Alonzo Bemis, is a three story edifice, located about one hundred rods from the Lake and commanding a fine view of it. There is a large piazza extending around the house and a promenade deck along the roof. The house is well arranged. The sleeping rooms are spacious; the parlors well furnished; and the tables well provided. Fish abound in the Lake and especially the *muscalunge*, a species of pickerel peculiar to the Lake.

LAKE MEMPHREMAGOG

is another beautiful sheet of water, much larger and somewhat farther to the north than Willoughby. It is on the line between Canada and Vermont. The distance thither from Willoughby is eighteen miles—the first seven of which may be accomplished, if desired, by boat. From thence a stage runs to the Lake.

Memphremagog is thirty-five miles long and from one to six wide. Its general course is north and south. Black River, Barton River, and the Clyde flow into it from Vermont. It receives the waters of several small streams in Lower Canada and empties, through Magog River, into the St. Francis and thence into the St. Lawrence. It contains some islands of considerable size and great loveliness. There are several towns and villages of respectable population along its shores.

OWL'S HEAD MT., 2,743 feet high, rises up on the western side, and affords, from its summit, a view more extended and magnificent than almost any other in this portion of New England. A bridle path has recently been constructed to the summit. Lake Champlain, Massaweepee Lake, and Lake Willoughby, the White Mountains and the Green Mountains, the rivers St. Lawrence and St. Francis can be clearly seen. In a fair day the city of Montreal is also visible. Aside from these more remote views, there is a most enchanting prospect at its very base, along the entire length of the Lake.

The steamboat "Mountain Maid" has been enlarged the past year to double its former size. It runs from Newport in Vermont to Outlet Village in Canada, touching at different places on the Lake, under the command of Capt. FOGG. There are several good Hotels in these various places. The MOUNTAIN HOUSE, near Owl's Head, is as comfortable as any and as well kept.

2. FRANCONIA via PLYMOUTH. The traveller, as we said before, may leave the cars at Plymouth and proceed directly

up the valley of the Pemigewasset to Franconia. This is, by far, the shortest and most direct route to this part of the mountain region. The distance from Boston to Franconia is 145 miles; from Concord, 75. The time from Boston is ten hours. Leaving New York by the evening boats, one may be in Franconia in season for tea the next day. Fare, from Boston, $6.00; from Concord, $3.85.

Leaving Concord in the cars as indicated on page 116, we arrive at Plymouth in season for dinner. There are many objects of interest at Plymouth, if one desires to remain and become acquainted with the charms of the locality — BURNHAM'S HOTEL is a desirable tarrying place for all in quest of health or pleasure. Plymouth Village has a lovely situation, in the midst of the finest scenery. From Walker's Hill, can be obtained a capital view of the village and the river. Livermore's Falls, two miles north of the village, present a remarkable appearance. They are probably the result of volcanic action, and invite the attention of the student of science, and the lover of nature. Prospect Hill affords an unsurpassed view of the most diversified character. Mountain, valley, lake, and river, interspersed with fertile meadows, shining cottages, and thrifty villages, within a circuit of thirty miles, meet the delighted eye in every direction, while in the north the rugged cliffs and peaks of the Franconia and White Mountain ranges rise like everlasting towers. This is the finest view, with the exception of Red Hill, south of the mountains. The distance, from the hotel, is, by carriage, three miles, and one additional mile of bridle-path. Devil's Den is a cave from three hundred to four hundred feet deep, and is situated in Campton Hollow, six miles distant from Plymouth. Good trout-fishing may be found at Waterville, eighteen miles distant. Board may be obtained in Plymouth at the PEMIGEWASSET HOUSE at the rate of $1.00 and $1.50 per day; in private families for $4 and $5.00 per week. If the traveller desires to be independent of stagecoaches and railroads, he can obtain horses and drivers at the livery stables in the village.

Should he choose the stage-coach, he will enjoy a most delightful ride of twenty-four miles to the FLUME HOUSE, tracing the course of the Pemigewasset River. The road in some places is rather rough, but the weariness of the way is amply compensated by the variety of beautiful objects, that are everywhere presented to the view. The river meanders in its winding course, now with placid and quiet current through green meadows, and now in rapid and headlong torrent over its pebbly bed, while little cascades are bursting from the hills, falling in sheeted foam over the opposing rocks, to make their way to the welcoming stream below. As the route leaves the village, the mountains begin to appear in the distance. As the distance lessens, the white porticos of the Flume House are seen, welcoming our approach. The hotel seems like a "nest among the mountains," as it is relieved by the dark mass, amid which it rests. The little villages of Campton and Thornton are the resort of artists, who spend weeks in the vicinity sketching for future studies. Campton is said to contain more points for fine prospects, than any town in the neighborhood. A quiet little inn upon the roadside looks the abode of comfort. Woodstock and Lincoln are small towns of no particular note. The road is now in the midst of the mountain region. The dark hills loom up on every side, as the day departs. The Pemigewasset, now reduced to a little brook, murmurs at our feet. We have seen the summits of the hills brighten in the rich glow of sunset. The clouds are tinged with golden light, changing to soft purple, and the grey of evening. The stars come out, the moon sends her gentle rays down into the valley. In the late twilight, after a half day's exquisite enjoyment, we climb the hill and soon alight beneath the grateful shelter of the FLUME HOUSE. The PROFILE HOUSE is in the same region, four miles distant, and passengers who desire, can immediately proceed thither.

3. White Mountain Notch via Conway, Centre Harbor, Lake Winnipisaukee, and Concord. Distance from Boston, 172 miles. Time, 36 hours. Fare, $7.50.

At the Weirs, (32 miles from Concord; 106 from Boston; and 73 from White Mountain Notch) we leave the cars of the Boston, Concord & Montreal Railroad (see page 116) and find ourselves on

Lake Winnipisaukee.

The Lake lies in the two counties of Carroll and Belknap, and is very irregular in form. At the west end, as we approach it at the Weirs, it is divided into three large bays; at the north is a fourth; and at the east end there are three others. Its general course is from southeast to northwest. From one extreme end to the other the distance is not far from twenty-five miles. The width varies from one to seven miles. The towns of Moultonborough, Wolf borough, Tuftonborough, Centre Harbor, Meredith, Gilford and Alton, lie upon its borders, while from the high land of more distant towns fine views can be obtained of its placid waters.

The waters of the Lake descend four hundred and seventy-two feet in finding their way to the Atlantic. A rapid river of its own name, over which the railroad passes at Sanbornton Bridge, serves as its outlet to the Merrimack. The depths of Lake Winnipisaukee are remarkably clear, so that the fish can be seen with great distinctness, playing among the stones at the depth of many feet. The fish, of which there is a great variety, can be frequently caught at the steamboat wharf. While the boat is waiting for the arrival of the trains it is no uncommon thing for the passengers to employ their leisure hours in keeping Capt. Walker's fishing tackle from rusting for want of use. The "oldest inhabitants," who know the haunts "where *fish* do congregate," can convey you to rare sport. There is one place, and one only, in the Lake where for about two weeks large numbers of smelts can be caught. Then all disappear and none are seen till the recurrence of the same season. Formerly, before so many dams obstructed their course, the shad came up here from the sea to leave their spawn in the shallow bays. The progress of manufactures has now greatly abridged their ancient privileges.

Lake Winnipisaukee is a mountain lake. Yet it lacks almost all those wild rough features of mountain scenery which usually characterize inland waters in mountainous regions. The mountains rise on all sides, but the shore seen from the distance is compartively smooth and level. The islands, far from being precipitous and rocky, are covered with verdure and seem to float like fairy castles upon the broad lake-mirror. The lake is usually approached in the calm and stillness of the noon-day sun. The spirit of repose, incident upon the hour and upon the escape from the hot, dusty cars, harmonizes with the green foliage of the islands and the quiet surface of the water. By and by, just after starting, a mild, balmy breeze just ruffles the surface of the lake, and giving yourself up to its softening influences, you no longer wonder at the Indian admiration which gave it the name of "The beautiful water in a high place."

The Lake, in common with Lake George and Casco Bay, has its three hundred and sixty-five islands, and, perhaps an extra one for leap year. Indeed it would be a modification of the old tale if in future Lake Winnipisaukee should claim three hundred and sixty-six for leap years and leave to its rivals the more vulgar tradition.

At the WEIRS, we embark upon the steamboat "THE LADY OF THE LAKE." This is a charming little steamer and under the safe protection of Capt. WM. WALKER, JR,, you will ride safely to Centre Harbor or Wolf borough. Near the Weirs, at the head of the river, had you time, you might see the old "Endicott Rock" with its quaint and curious carving. It was discovered a few years since by accident as they were building a dam. It is supposed to commemorate the following: In 1652, during the administration of Gov. Endicott, the General Court of Massachusetts, desirous of more exactly ascertaining the bounds of their colony, appointed Captains Edward Johnson and Simon Willard commissioners for the purpose of making a survey. The expedition which they headed, reached this spot, where their Indian guide assured them the Merrimack had its head waters. The E I and S W are the initials of the early surveyors; the W P is considered an abbreviation of "Worshipful." The remainder probably alludes to the fact that the expedition was undertaken during the administration of Worshipful Gov. John Endicott.

But the tinkling of the signal bell soon gives us warning that we are to leave the wharf. We now wind our way through the numberless islands that crowd our path. Red Hill now appears in sight and then is lost behind an intervening island. An opening between two islands give you a view of Rattlesnake Island. The snake after which the island is named is even now to be found here. None have been seen elsewhere about the lake for many years. Gunstock Mountain is also to be

View of "Aunt Dolly's."

seen on the right, and on the opposite quarter Ossipee rears its bare head. This mountain, the tourist will find difficulty in escaping. The road towards the Notch winds round its base, and not till he has passed over a good part of his journey toward Conway, will he succeed in leaving it behind him. About three miles from the Weirs we reach Bear Island, which is nearly four miles long. Upon one of these numerous islands there resided, in 1851, "solitary and alone," an aged spinster familiarly known as "Aunt Dolly." In this wild and romantic spot, almost entirely cut off from the world, she lived in hermit grandeur, taking care of her corn, her few sheep, and occasionally rowing her own skiff to the main land. At length, after a ride of ten miles, we reach CENTRE HARBOR.

Should the traveller have leisure to spend upon this beautiful Lake, he cannot do better than continue his journey to

WOLFBOROUGH.

The distance from Centre Harbor is about twenty miles, and is usually accomplished in two hours. For the first mile or two the course pursued is the same as that over which he has just passed. But we soon leave the old path and pass through a broader portion of the Lake than that just traversed. It is a most delightful trip in a clear morning or pleasant evening. At sunset, particularly, and when the evening shades begin to prevail, we have the finest view of the distant mountains, with their ever varying hues.

If it falls to the lot of the traveller to be near the Lake on some bright moonlight evening, he should not fail to inquire if a moonlight excursion is to take place. These excursions are frequently made by parties from neighboring towns who charter the boat for that purpose. They even come, at times, from Concord and from Dover on extra trains. A ticket for the excursion can easily be obtained, and it will not be deemed an intrusion. Rather than attempt any suggestion of the beauties of the Lake at such a time, we leave it to be actually realized or imagined.

The village at Wolfborough is delightfully situated on two beautiful slopes of land rising from a bay of the Lake. The "Pavillion," a spacious and comfortable hotel is situated on the rising ground, commanding a fine view of the Lake. Horses and carriages can be obtained at the livery stables. Boats, for fishing parties or sailing excursions are also obtainable.

Copple Crown Mountain, five miles from Wolfborough may be easily ascended. The view from its summit is thought by many to equal that from Red Hill. The mountain scenery is, however, more distant. The prospect embraces an excellent view of the Lake, a large number of villages, and some thirty sheets of water in New Hampshire and Maine can be counted. Vessels on the ocean can be discerned with a glass. Adjoining Copple Crown, on the northeast, is a smaller mountain of singular formation, called "Tumble-down-Dick." Mt. Washington may be distinctly discerned in a clear day.

The price of board is from $5.00 to $10.00 per week.

Leaving Wolfborough we return by the steamer to

Centre Harbor. This beautiful summer retreat is situated on the northern shore of the Lake, between Winnipisaukee and Squam Lake. Its fine location and beautiful scenery have long made it a favorite resort for those accustomed to frequent the Lake. The fine excursions, which can be made along the shores of the Lake — around the "ring," skirting on Squam Lake—or to Red Hill, render it very attractive. Good boats are also to be had for fishing parties upon the Lake.

The Senter House, by Gilman & Huntress, formerly of the Profile House, is a large and pleasant hotel. It is situated on the rising ground facing the Lake, of which it commands an excellent view. The hotel, one of the best in the mountain region, is commodious and well furnished, and has been long and favorably known for the convenience of its arrangements, the perfection of its table, and courtesy of the proprietors. An extensive livery stable is connected with the hotel. Moulton's Hotel is a smaller house near by.

The chief object of interest in the immediate vicinity of Centre Harbor is

Red Hill.

From this hill, about four miles distant, in Moultonborough, the best view of the Lake and the circumjacent scenery can be obtained. Its height, two thousand five hundred feet, places before the eye of the observer an extensive, varied, and picturesque tract of country, perhaps nowhere excelled in New England. It is by no means difficult to climb. There is a wagon-path to the base, and thence well trained ponies convey you to the summit. The top is destitute of trees and bushes, and affords an uninterrupted prospect far and wide. In clear days the peaks of the White Mountains are dimly discernable in the far north; the Ossipee Mountains appear in the east; a little to the north, Chocorua, recalling its Indian tradition, rears its craggy summit; and still farther away the mountains of Maine close in the view. Kearsarge and Monadnock are plainly visible at the southwest, with Gunstock at the southeast. Squam Lake, six miles long, is glittering in the sunshine on the west.

But to the south and east lies Winnipisaukee, the gem of all New England Lakes. The ascent of Red Hill is usually made in the forenoon; but to enjoy the exquisite loveliness of Winnipisaukee it should be made in the afternoon or in the early morning. In the middle of the day the blinding glare of the sun upon the water almost robs it of the quiet beauty of its softness and harmony. But in the afternoon the sun illumines with a genial glow the calm expanse of the distant surface of the Lake; the rippling waves just reflect its image; the hundred islands assume their peculiar form of grace and loveliness; the mountains on the opposite shore, from a glow of crimson, change to a brown purple, as the lingering rays of the setting sun leave them, one by one; while the advancing shadows of those nearer to you change to a new form the fairy outline of the Lake. If, too, you are early riser enough to see, from its summit, the sun roll up majestically from behind the opposite hills, you will acknowledge that Lake Winnipisaukee possesses a charm and beauty peculiar to itself.

Coaches leave Centre Harbor for Conway regularly every day soon after the arrival of the morning boat from the Weirs. Ample time is allowed for dining on the boat, or, after landing, at the excellent hotel just spoken of. The distance to Conway is thirty miles, and the fare from Centre Harbor $2.50.

MOULTONBOROUGH, five miles from Centre Harbor, contains Red Hill. Ossipee Mountain, moreover, extends into it. On that part of the mountain, within the limits of the town are two springs of some note; the one a mineral chalybeate spring, sovereign for cutaneous diseases; the other simply a spring of good cold water, sovereign for thirstiness, sixteen feet in diameter, and through the centre of which the water, containing a quantity of fine white sand, is thrown up two feet. From this source flows a beautiful stream, which, about a mile below, has a perpendicular descent of about seventy feet. On its left side is a cave containing relics of Indian life. Many of these relics have been found in various parts of the town, and it is probable that the Ossipee tribe of Indians had their residence near here.

SANDWICH is a small rocky town, merely touched upon in one corner. White Face Mountain in this town is 2,970 feet high. It is visible from the road. The course of a land-slide which occurred about thirty years ago can easily be traced on the south side. At Centre Sandwich, a few miles from the main road, the traveller will find neat and quiet accommodation at the hotel kept by James H. Durgin. Squam Lake is quite near the hotel and the mountain brooks abound in trout. The price of board is from $3.00 to $10.00 per week.

TAMWORTH is sixteen miles from Centre Harbor. Thence coasting along the shores of Ossipee Pond, a beautiful sheet of water lying in the town of Madison, after a drive of fourteen miles Conway is reached. Ossipee signifies "Pine River." The Pond is also sometimes called Pequawket Lake.

In this latter part of the drive, a fine view is obtained of Mt. Chocorua ("The old bear.") It is one of the most notable of the lower peaks of the White Mountain range. It is 3,358 feet high and without vegetation—other than such as a few blueberries or cranberries create. It is, in fact, a granite mountain, with pinnacles and precipices, sharp, angular peaks and unexpected descents;—a countless myriad of great boulders, hurled together by more than Titanic force. One of the peaks of Chocorua is the scene of the tragic incident from which the peak derives its name, so beautifully narrated by Mrs. Seba Smith.

CONWAY, though the gate to the mountain region, is one of the most level towns in the State. In itself it possesses few objects of interest. In the vicinity, however, are brooks well stocked with trout. Most of the objects of interest in North Conway, also, are accessible from this place. Here, however, the stage remains over night. The CONWAY HOUSE, kept by JONATHAN DOW, is an excellent hotel. It is particularly famous for its omelettes, which will be found very palatable after the ride from Centre Harbor.

From Conway to Gibb's Hotel the distance is thirty-three miles. The fare is $2.50. The road, though hilly and broken, affords charming landscape views.

Five miles farther on, in the valley of the Saco, and surrounded on all sides by mountains, lies

NORTH CONWAY, the favorite resort of our New England Artists. Many families resort to this place in the summer season to avoid the noise, bustle and expense of large hotels. The Saco river here is from ten to twelve rods wide, and usually about two feet deep. It has been known to rise 27, and even 30 feet in twenty-four hours. Large quantities of magnesia and fullers' earth are found in the town. Three good hotels are located here; the WASHINGTON HOUSE, by W. C. EASTMAN, is three stories high and will accommodate about seventy-five; the KEARSARGE HOUSE, by SAMUEL W. THOMPSON; and the NORTH CONWAY HOUSE, by N. R. MASON. Echo Lake, Diana's Bath, the Cathedral, White Horse and Hart's Ledge are places much visited and within three hours ride. Kearsarge or Pequawket mountain, 3,367 feet above sea level, is an object of interest. The hotel erected on the summit has almost fallen to decay. The view of the mountains from North Conway is very charming. The accompanying engraving may serve to give one an idea of the scene.

A pleasant ride of ten miles brings us to

UPPER BARTLETT. At this point we join the travel between the Glen House and Gibb's. For a further description see page 45.

V. NEW YORK TO CONCORD, N. H., by way of Worcester, Nashua and Manchester. The traveller may leave New York in the morning by route No. IV, page 95, and go to Worcester. From Worcester he will proceed to Nashua and arrive at Concord at 8 P. M. and leave for the mountains by routes above at 10:30 the next morning. Distance 275 miles. Fare, $6.50. Or he may leave in the evening over the same route or by the boat to Allyn's Point, route No. III, page 93, and, waiting at Worcester till morning, proceed to Concord, arriving in season to go to the mountains by the same trains as before. Fare by boat, $5.00.

It is in contemplation, during the present season, to run a passenger car the entire distance between Allyn's Point and Littleton by the way of Worcester, Nashua, Concord, Weirs and Plymouth. A return car, to connect with the boat for New York, will also leave Littleton and go all the way to Allyn's Point. By this arrangement, the traveller will leave

View of the White Mountains from North Conway.

New York in the evening, step on board the cars at Allyn's Point, proceed, with a short detention at Worcester, over the whole of his journey by rail, to the Weirs, to Plymouth, or to Littleton in the same car. Returning he will go *without any change of cars* directly to the steamboat at Allyn's Point. Much confusion and trouble will thus be avoided.

Should the preference be given to the Railroad line, the traveller will take the cars of the New York and New Haven Railroad, which skirts the northern shore of Long Island Sound. For a distance of seventy-six miles, it passes through numerous agricultural villages and the busy cities of NORWALK and BRIDGEPORT. The cars leave the passenger station on Twenty seventh street at the advertised time.

WILLIAMS BRIDGE is the junction with the Harlem Railroad. EAST CHESTER, NEW ROCHELLE, MAMARONECK and RYE, are small villages in the State of New York. The road crosses the State line into Connecticut, soon after leaving PORT CHESTER. GREENWICH, STAMFORD, and DARIEN are pleasant, agricultural and maritime towns in the "land of steady habits." NORWALK will be painfully remembered as the scene of the distressing accident, which occurred on this Road a few years ago, the cars running off the track through the open draw of the bridge across the Norwalk river, and maiming and killing several persons. We gladly leave this place behind us, and hurry on through WESTPORT, SOUTHPORT, and FAIRFIELD, all quiet, cheerful towns, to the fine city of BRIDGEPORT. This place has a large fishing and coasting interest, and considerable manufactures. Here the Housatonic Railroad forms a junction with the New Haven Road, and offers a beautiful avenue of travel through the exquisite scenery of western Connecticut and Massachusetts. Passing on, we go rapidly through STRATFORD, (the junction of the Naugatuck Railroad,) MILFORD, and WEST HAVEN, to NEW HAVEN, which is one of the finest cities of New England. A stroll through the quiet streets, enshadowed by thousands of graceful elms, and lined with comfortable, and, in some instances, palatial residences, intermingled with ivy-covered churches, is most satisfactory and enjoyable. The visitor will notice the (Yale) College Green and buildings, and the State House. The Canal Railroad connects New Haven with *Northampton* by a rival route to the Springfield and Hartford Road. The New Haven and New London Railroad furnishes a route to Providence, a small steamboat plying between New London and Stonington, connecting at the latter with Stonington and Providence Railroad.

Leaving New Haven, we pass quickly through North Haven, Wallingford, Meriden, Berlin, and Newington, which is the station for Wethersfield, — over whose vegetable productions many tears have been vainly shed, — to

Hartford. This is a much more busy and bustling place, than its twin sister, which we have just left. Here also is a State House, for Connecticut, in common with Rhode Island, rejoices in two capitals. The reason of it must be traced to colonial prejudice. The two settlements were formerly under different govérnments, and when they were united into one State, it was found necessary to establish two places of government, to satisfy both parties. Among the public buildings, may be noticed the Asylum for the Deaf and Dumb, the Retreat for the Insane, and Trinity College, all handsome establishments. Some of the most elegant and expensive Churches in New England are found in this city. The Trumbull Gallery and Library is worth a visit. Hartford is the residence of Mrs. Sigourney, and, was at one time, that of Andrew Jackson Davis. A cultivated and intelligent society makes the place attractive, both for strangers and residents. The Allyn House, a new and elegant Hotel, occupies a fine site, a short distance from the depot, and is a model house of entertainment.

At this point, we come into the valley of the Connecticut, which, for those who leave this route at Springfield and go by the way of Bellow's Falls, will be in sight for a great part of the time, till they arrive at Well's River, Vt. Stopping for a moment at WINDSOR, we cross the river at WINDSOR LOCKS, a busy village, thence through ENFIELD and THOMPSONVILLE, we cross the State line into Massachusetts at LONGMEADOW, one of the best farming towns in western Massachusetts. It is only four miles farther to

SPRINGFIELD. The MASSASOIT HOUSE and the RUSSELL HOUSE are both first class houses near the depot. If the traveller desires to remain over night, or for a longer time, he will find no more comfortable place anywhere than at these hotels. The United States Armory is about a mile distant, and will well repay the trouble of a visit, while the city itself, with its nice, well shaded streets, its fine residences, and its agreeable social life, will furnish many inducements for a prolonged stay. To those, going up the valley of the Connecticut, a short stop is allowed for dinner. The passenger for Concord now passes through the centre of Massachusetts, a fine agricultural district, to

WORCESTER. Here we join the line of travel from New York, via Allyn's Point, described. From Worcester our route lies over the Worcester and Nashua Railroad which passes through a number of small towns, of considerable thrift. From WEST BOYLSTON to STERLING JUNCTION, Mt. Wachusett, eight miles distant, may be observed, in a westerly direction. At Sterling Junction, a portion of the train branches to Fitchburg, giving passengers an opportunity to proceed to the valley of the Connecticut, over the Cheshire Railroad.

CLINTON is a busy manufacturing town.

LANCASTER is a delightful village, affording many fine views from various points. At STILL RIVER an excellent view of the surrounding country is obtained. HARVARD STATION is at some distance from the town, which stands high and is much esteemed for a quiet summer residence.

GROTON JUNCTION is a quiet enough place at any other time than upon the arrival of the cars. Then it is a scene of great disorder. Six trains simultaneously arrive and depart over the Fitchburg, Worcester & Nashua, Stony Brook (for Lowell) and Peterboro' & Shirley Railroads. Old ladies with brown paper parcels and umbrellas, young ladies with band-boxes, fond parents with frightened babies, bewildered old gentlemen, and smart young dandies, who are too knowing to inquire, and invariably go wrong, polite conductors, and hurrying express carriers, are mingled in almost inextricable confusion. But the railway officials are patient and attentive, and do their best to prevent mistakes. Those unfortunates, who are always making blunders, should by all means, avoid Groton Junction. We advise the traveller to keep his seat, his baggage check, and his equanimity, and be grateful when the train is fairly under way again, and this babel is seen no more.

GROTON, PEPPERELL and HOLLIS are agricultural towns, located on elevated ground, and present from different prominent points, some exceedingly pretty pictures.

We at length reach NASHUA, and the continuation of the route is the same as described on the 109th and following pages.

VI. NEW YORK TO FRANCONIA, via Springfield and Bellows Falls. Distance to Bellows Falls, 222 miles; fare $6.00. Cars leave New York at 8 o'clock, A. M.; arrive at Bellows Falls at 6 o'clock, P. M., stopping at Springfield half an hour for dinner. Railroads: New York & New Haven; New Haven & Springfield; Connecticut River; Vermont Valley.

From New York to Springfield, the route is the same as described on the 134th and following pages. At Springfield, we take the cars of the Connecticut River Railroad, and continue up the valley of the river.

The Connecticut River Railroad extends from Springfield to South Vernon, Vt., and passes through Cabotville, Chicopee,

Willimansett, three busy manufacturing villages; then crossing to the west bank of the river, into the new city of Holyoke, it winds along under the shadow of Mt. Tom, 1,200 feet high, to Northampton, which is like a Paradise in its rural charms and graces. A noted Water Cure Establishment, at Round Hill, commanding an entensive view, is located in this town. Amherst College is seven miles distant, on the opposite side of the river, and Mt. Holyoke near it, 830 feet above the river, is distinctly seen. The route passes on through Hatfield, Whately, South Deerfield, and Deerfield, containing the finest farms and meadows of this section, across the Deerfield River to

Greenfield, a smart, busy, thriving place. Should the tourist desire to stop a while here, he will find a good home at the Mansion House. One of the most popular places of resort for the town's people is The Glen, a most lovely, retired spot, just beyond the town line, in the town of Lyndon. Turner's Falls, in the Connecticut, in the neighborhood of which are to be found the gigantic "bird-tracks," familiar to geologists, are about four miles distant, over a good road. Leaving Greenfield, the Railroad passes through Bernardston, to South Vernon, on the boundary line of Vermont. Here an opportunity is presented of visiting Keene, the most important town in southwestern New Hampshire, by taking the cars of the Ashuelot Railroad, passing through the small towns of Hinsdale, the residence of the present Governor of the State, Winchester, and Swanzey. From Keene, the traveller can proceed over the Cheshire Railroad, to Bellows Falls, through East Westmoreland, Westmoreland and Walpole, within sight of Mt. Monadnock. Should he choose not to diverge at South Vernon, he will take the cars of the Vermont Valley Railroad, and will soon reach Brattleboro', famous for its fine Water Cure, the purity and salubrity of its climate, its agreeable society, and the marvellous beauty of the surrounding scenery. Chesterfield Mountain, on the New Hampshire bank of the Connecticut, is a favorite place of resort. From an observatory on its summit, a wide panorama is to be seen, closed by the peaks of the White Hills in the northern distance. Brattleboro' furnishes the most numerous attractions for a summer residence of any town in this vicinity. Thence the road lies through Dummerston—the site of a military fortress in the Revolution, called Fort Dummer—Putney, East Putney, and Westminster. At 6 o'clock, P. M. the traveller will be very glad to step from the cars at

BELLOWS FALLS, distant from New York, 222 miles. This is a delightfully situated village, on the Vermont side of the Connecticut River. The ISLAND HOUSE, a short distance from the station, occupies a favorable site. It is a new, and well built structure, and furnishes a quiet home either for the invalid or the pleasure seeker. Directly in the rear, rises a lofty hill, presenting a fine view from its summit, which is easily reached. There is also a view obtainable from the bridge over the Connecticut in this place, well worthy of the tourist's attention. The river, which above is deep, broad and tranquil, with a width of about a thousand feet, and which below expands to an equal or greater surface, is, at this spot, beneath the bridge, compressed within a channel not more than twenty feet wide. Through this channel—confined on either side by a high granite wall, the whole volume of the Connecticut is forced, with a power and rapidity, which whitens its waters like a tide of snow-flakes. The fall is in no place perpendicular but in the distance of half a mile the waters descend forty-two feet. These falls were formerly a favorite resort of the Indians for purposes of fishing. Salmon were caught here in great numbers till within a recent period. Just below the bridge, on the west side of the river, will be noticed a large flat rock, covered with hieroglyphics and rude portraits, supposed to have been cut by the aboriginal frequenters of this place.

On the following morning, we proceed north over the Sullivan Railroad, leaving Bellows Falls about noon. Charlestown is a good farming town, well situated on the eastern bank of the Connecticut, which the road has crossed at Bellows Falls. Claremont is a pleasant manufacturing village on a small stream, emptying into the Connecticut. There are several cotton, woollen, and paper mills, besides other manufacturing establishments. Eleven miles farther the road again crosses the river, and brings the tourist to

WINDSOR, VT. As the cars run up the valley, the traveller will notice Mt. Ascutney, on the Vermont side, 3,200 feet high, and of easy ascent. Along the banks of the river and at the base of the hills, the eye will be gratified with the sight of numerous neat and pleasant farm houses, whose outward appearance betokens the comfort and happiness of their inmates. Windsor is a place of considerable size and prominence. The Vermont State Prison is located here, and has obtained considerable reputation for the excellent quality of the fire-arms of various kinds manufactured by the inmates.

Taking the cars of the Vermont Central Railroad, we continue our journey through Hartland and North Hartland, to White River Junction. The remainder of this route is the same as described on the 112th and following pages.

VII. NEW YORK TO FRANCONIA, via North River and Bellows Falls, Vt. Distance to Bellows Falls, 287 miles. Leave by boat or railroad 6:30, and 7, A. M.; arrive at Rutland, 9, P. M. Leave Rutland, 5:45, A. M.; arrive at Bellows Falls 8:30, A. M. Fares by boat to Albany, $5; by rail, $7. Railroads: Hudson River; Washington & Rutland or Western Vermont; Rutland and Burlington.

The Hudson River has sometimes been called the Rhine of America. Intelligent and unprejudiced foreigners have pronounced the American stream superior to the European in every respect. It is navigable a much longer distance for vessels of considerable size; its scenery is more varied, and there is more life and action along its banks. If it wants the addition of castles crowning the summits of the adjacent hills, the absence is more to be wished for than their presence. They are associated with times of barbarism, oppression, and the cruelty of feudal war. Our hills, reposing in the sunlight, or dark with the passage of storm clouds, are dear to us, from the associations which they have with the triumphs of liberty. Almost every point, from New York through the Highlands, even to Albany, has its history as connected with our revolutionary struggle. The interest which gathers around our recollections of Washington and his soldiers adds to the inspiring influence, which the contemplation of the natural beauties of the region excites. Our eyes rest on the same scenes, which our great captain loved to gaze upon. Our feet may tread the same paths, along which he rode in anxious thought, or in the fore-consciousness of victory. Every true patriot must be proud of the Hudson.

We remember, too, that it was upon this river, that the first successful experiment in steam navigation was made by Fulton. He bravely persevered in his project of sailing, by means of steam, against the scoffs and jeers of all his friends, and when his boat left the pier, and made her way against the tide up the beautiful river, he had the joy of exciting, even among the most incredulous, the wildest enthusiasm of admiration. It is related that the crews of the vessels which he passed, as the strange bark approached them, with its volumes of smoke and its noisy machinery, were overwhelmed with affright. "They shrank from their decks at the terrific sight, and left their vessels to go ashore, while others prostrated themselves and besought Providence to protect them from the approach of the horrible monster, that was marching on the tide, and lighting its path by the fire which it vomited." The world has moved since then.

For the journey to Albany, the summer tourist has his choice of travel. If he desires speed, he can step on board the comfortable Hudson River Railroad cars and run his own risk of sight-seeing. If he wishes to enjoy the scenery, and is not so timid, as the "unprotected female," who would not step foot upon a steamboat, till the runner assured her, that his "boat had no boiler and so there was no danger of explosion"—let him select some fine day, and take one of the day boats to Albany. For the modest sum of seventy-five cents, he can have a four hours' sail to WEST POINT, passing under the shadows of the Palisades, and through a large portion of the Highlands.

On leaving New York, he will notice, upon the opposite bank, which belongs to the State of New Jersey—the busy JERSEY CITY, and the charming HOBOKEN, and just above the duelling ground of Burr and Hamilton. FORT LEE still on the New Jersey side is at the beginning of the PALISADES. These are composed of a wonderful formation of basaltic or trap rock, are in height from two to five hundred feet, and extend with their frowning precipices, within a few feet of the water's edge, for a distance of twenty-five miles along the western bank of the river. This countinuous line of perpendicular cliffs is a most remarkable object. Underneath them, on the small strip of beach, may occasionally be seen a little village of two or three houses, with a landing place for the passing vessels. An occasional ravine, leading up the steep side of the bluff furnishes carriage communication with the interior. In some instances, no such communication exists, and the scanty inhabitants depend entirely upon the river for connection with the outside world. The summits of the Palisades are well wooded with a luxuriant growth of various kinds of trees, Just beyond, in the immediate interior, and at a considerable elevation above the river is the famous Rockland Pond, which supplies a large part of New York City with the purest ice. The view from the summit of the Palisades is superb. On a clear afternoon, the passing sails upon Long Island Sound can be discerned in the distance, while in the foreground, a long reach of the North River, from the Bay to the Tappan Zee, the rich farms of Westchester county, and the fine country seats of the New York millionaires upon the opposite banks, with the picturesque appearance of the small steamers plying to and from the city and its suburbs, the numerous sloops and schooners, with the sun glistening on their wings, as they go and come, combine to form a picture, which, when once seen, is unfadingly daguerreotyped upon the memory. The tourist, however, is on board the steamboat, and this view is denied him. In default of it, we point out to him MANHATTANVILLE, with its green lawns and pleasant residences; FORT WASHINGTON, a memorable place in the Revolution; and a structure in the form of a castle, built of stone, the erection of Mr. Edwin Forrest. To a man more interested in the movements of the present day, than in attempts to reproduce the past, the arrangement for the conveyance of the telegraphic wires from the island, upon which the city of New York is situated, to the West and South will be of much greater interest. An immensely tall flagstaff, secured by numerous iron cables, rises upon the eastern bank of the river. From the top of this the wires are suspended in mid-air across to a staff erected upon the Palisades. Part of the necessary wires are laid in the bed of the river across to the opposite side, and thus, the great business connections of New York with the country are established.

Passing onward, we reach YONKERS, a pleasant village upon the eastern bank of the river, the residence of "Mr. Sparrowgrass," whose beautiful and commodious dwelling hardly suggests the ludicrous inconveniences of "living in the country." Four miles farther is DOBBS' FERRY, which has its historical reminiscences. Opposite this place, a few miles above, is PIERMONT, the freight terminus of the New York and Erie Railroad. A massive pier, a mile in length, extends into the river, on which are built the railroad tracks, and the immense freight depots, necessary for the great business of the road.

On the eastern bank, a mile or two above Dobbs' Ferry, is SUNNY SIDE, the residence of WASHINGTON IRVING. The house can just be discerned, peeping through the luxuriant foliage that embowers it. It is a home for a poet. Before the railroad was built, the lawn extended to the river side, and a little creek making up immediately below, gave the estate a situation like a little cape. It was a great annoyance to the quiet student, to have his place invaded by the "march of improvement," and he expressed the wish, that he "might have been born after the world was fairly finished."

We now enter upon the TAPPAN ZEE, passing on the East, SING SING, the location of the famous New York State Prison, and on the West, the village of NYAK, where Major Andre was executed. We pass quickly, through the fleet of vessels which covers the waters of Tappan Zee, and enter upon the Highlands through HAVERSTRAW BAY. In rapid succession we see on the west, the villages of HAVERSTRAW, GRASSY POINT, STONY POINT, with the old Fort Clinton. Opposite Stony Point, is VERPLANCK POINT. Above, on the east, is the picturesque village of PEEKSKILL, and we are now in the beautiful region of the HIGHLANDS. The hills rise abruptly from the water, the steamer in some instances passing within biscuit throw of the shore. The slopes are covered with verdure, and fine trees, prominent among which is a beautiful species of cedar, growing with its lower limbs close to the soil, and rising in conical form, affording a most pleasing object in the landscape. Some of the hills are almost perpendicular precipices, where the foot of man has scarcely trod. The heights seem impregnable, and Washington showed his consummate generalship, in fortifying these strong positions, and making the Hudson the base of his operations in the North through the whole Revolutionary war. Had the treachery of Arnold been successful, the issue of the struggle would have been most disastrous to the colonies. We are now drawing near to WEST POINT, our first landing place since leaving New York. As we approach the wharf, we see Cozzens' Hotel, a fine building overlooking the river, and occupying one of the finest sites for its purposes, to be found in the region. At the landing place are omnibusses to convey passengers to the different hotels. If one wishes to reach West Point by railroad, he must purchase a ticket for Garrison's, where he will find a small steam ferry boat, to convey him across the river. The route by railroad passes through the villages enumerated, on the east bank, and follows the river in all its windings, passing through tunnels of solid rock, and over bridges of massive strength. Some of the views obtained from the several points, which jut into the river, are exceedingly fine, and will convince the traveller that whether he goes by rail or boat, the trip up the Hudson is most delightful.

West Point has a national interest, as the site of the United States Military Academy, for the training of officers for the United States Army. The village is pleasantly situated in a basin formed by the depression of the land between the river on the east, and a semicircular range of hills on the west. It is almost completely separated from the outside world, and furnishes a most retired and excellent place for the purposes of its location. It is fifty-two miles from New York, and is reached in two hours and a half by rail, and three and a half hours by boat. Two good hotels furnish the traveller with the very best accommodations, at the price of $2.50 per day. Cozzens' Hotel is about a mile below the landing, and is a first-class house. Roe's Hotel, is somewhat nearer in a northerly direction, and has the additional advantage of being in the immediate vicinity of all the objects of interest. The parade ground of the Cadets is directly in front, and all the evolutions of the military drill in the Infantry, Cavalry, and Artillery service can be easily witnessed. During the months of July and August, with a portion of June and September, the Cadets live altogether in encampment, and the sojourner at Roe's will not be disagreeably disturbed from his morning slumbers, by the sound of the *réveillé*, almost beneath his windows. From the rear piazza of the hotel looking up the river is enjoyed a view of unsurpassed loveliness—being the reverse of that so familiar, looking down the river from Newburg. On the southern side of the Parade Ground, opposite the hotel, are ranged, the stone stables for the horses, and drill rooms, the Library, the residences of the Professors, and the barracks for the Cadets, the Arsenal and Laboratory. At the latter place may be seen some trophies of the Revolution, a brass mortar, captured at Stony Point, two smaller ones taken from Burgoyne, and a part of the chain, which Putnam stretched across the river to obstruct the passage of the British Ships of War. Above, are the ruins of Fort Putnam, which has so romantic and interesting a history, and from the summit of which an exquisite view is obtained. Not the least of the matters at West Point, which will interest the student of history, is the monument erected to Kosciusko, upon the eastern edge of the Parade. Among those which will interest our fair readers, are the tri-weekly hops at the Hall of the Academy, for the gratification of the Cadets and their numerous visitors.

Leaving West Point, where a most enjoyable visit may be made, we pass UNDERCLIFF, on the east, the residence of Geo. P. Morris, and IDLEWILD on the west, the residence of N. P. Willis. Then we stop a few moments at NEWBURG, a busy town, the residence of the late A. J. Downing. FISHKILL lies opposite, on the east bank. Farther on, is POUGHKEEPSIE, on the east side, a well built and pleasant town, with considerable trade, equidistant from Albany and New York, and beyond the Highlands. To compensate for the loss of these, the Cattskill Mountains begin to loom up in the distance. Snugly ensconced upon the side of one of the highest, may be seen the MOUNTAIN HOUSE, the finest hotel in the region. CATTSKILL LANDING is reached, from New York, about 2 o'clock, P. M., by boat;

Oakhill station by rail, with ferry across, somewhat earlier. A ride of four hours by stage, mostly ascending, through the regions of Rip Van Winkle, and affording most delightful glimpses, through the trees, of the widening prospect, brings the weary traveller to the hotel, which for neatness, elegance, beauty of situation, and all creature-comforts, is unequalled on the river. The view from the Table Rock, on which the house stands is most captivating. You look down a precipice, hundreds of feet in depth, and over the wide-lying, intervale farms on the plains below, to the noble Hudson, flecked with the white sails of passing vessels, while the mountains of Vermont and New Hampshire in the distance afford a fine background to the beautiful picture. The Catskill Falls are distant about a mile and a half from the hotel, and are well worth a visit. Price of board at hotel, $3.00 per day; Omnibus to Falls, 50 cents ; Stage from Steamboat Landing, $1.25.

Above Cattskill, there are villages lining the banks of the river. The most considerable place on the east side is Hudson, a city of some importance. Above this, are Columbia, Stuyvesant, and Kinderhook. Greenbush, opposite Albany, with which it connects by means of a ferry boat, is the terminus of the Hudson River Railroad proper, and, also, of the Western Railroad, between Boston and Albany.

Albany is the oldest city in the Union, with the exception of Jamestown, Va., but its antique appearance is gradually yielding to the progress of the time. Only a few relics remain. The most prominent objects in the city are the Capitol, on State St., the Museum, the Academy, Stanwix Hall, and the City Hall, the dome of which is imposingly gilded. There are some fine churches, and some fair hotels. The Delevan House, and Congress Hall have the widest reputation. Of these, the latter, though most distant from the landing must have the preference.

A few miles above Albany is Troy, on the East bank of the Hudson, and connected with its great rival, by ferry to

Greenbush, and thence by rail to Troy — the cars running at short intervals, and connecting immediately, at both places, with all the trains north, east, south and west. The railroad station at Troy is very commodious, and admirably arranged and managed. The city is very neat, and contains some fine churches, a Female Academy of some celebrity, and good hotels. Of these, the Troy House is the best. The Union, Mansion House, and American are to be ranked next. The last house, though not so fashionable as the others, has the reputation of cleanliness and comfort.

On the opposite shore is the United States Arsenal at Gibbonsville.

Leaving Troy, the traveller has a choice of two routes to RUTLAND, Vt.; one over the Troy & Boston Road to EAGLE BRIDGE, connecting there with the Rutland & Washington Railroad, or over the same road to NORTH BENNINGTON, connecting there with the Western Vermont Railroad. If he take the former, he will pass through LANSINGBURG, an exceedingly pleasant town; and, (after leaving Eagle Bridge, which is the place of junction for two or three railroads,) SALEM, a place of considerable importance. North of Salem, he will pass into the State of Vermont, and find himself amid all the beauties of the Green Mountains. The Great Haystack is in sight from this road. The track crosses the line again above PAWLET, Vt., and at MIDDLE GRANVILLE, the road is in New York. Four miles from this latter station, lies NORTH GRANVILLE, a most retired, pleasant, healthy, and picturesque village, the site of a Female Seminary of deserved reputation. Crossing again into Vermont, we stop a moment at CASTLETON, a lovely little village, the junction of the Whitehall and Saratoga Railroad; thence to Rutland, arriving if by morning train, about 1, P. M., if by evening train, at 9, P. M.

The route, over the Western Vermont Railroad, passes through SHAFTESBURY, ARLINGTON, and SUNDERLAND, all pleasant villages, to MANCHESTER, one of the finest towns in this section of Vermont. A capital hotel has been opened here within the last few years, called the Equinox House, and is beginning to be a place of great resort, on account of the natural beauties of the place, the fine drives in the neighborhood, and the reasonable prices for the excellent accommodations which are afforded. DORSET, WALLINGFORD, and CLARENDON have an air of comfort and quiet.

There is a third route from Troy to Rutland by way of SARATOGA, passing through BALLSTON. Leaving Saratoga by the Saratoga & Washington Railroad, the traveller passes through GANSEVOORT, MOREAN, FORT EDWARD, the site of a good Academy, FORT ANN, COMSTOCK'S, WHITEHALL, and HYDEVILLE to CASTLETON, there joining the Rutland & Washington Road. The times of arrival on all these routes are very nearly the same.

RUTLAND is the shire town of Rutland County and is one of the most important places of Central and Southern Vermont, containing about 4000 inhabitants. The central village is a thriving, comfortable place. The Bardwell House, situated very nearly opposite the Railroad Station, is a fine structure of brick, containing one hundred commodious rooms, and is altogether just such a home, as the tourist desires, after a hard day's travel. The charges are moderate; (per day, $2.00; per week, $7.00 to $10.50;) the table is well furnished and attended; the rooms are neat, clean and abundantly supplied; all substantial comforts are provided without offensive display. Situated as Rutland is, at the junction of four railroad routes, and within easy distance of Lakes Champlain and George, and almost in the midst of the mountains, it is a most desirable place for summer resort. The extensive Marble Quarries, the "Springs" at Clarendon, celebrated for their medicinal qualities, Sutherland Falls, called by Willis, "one of the loveliest places in the world," and Killington Peak nearly 4,000 feet high, the loftiest peak of the Green Mountains in this region, are all in the immediate vicinity, and can be visited at a small expense; while "mine host," Cooke, will see that in-door arrangements for good living are not wanting. The disciple of Isaak Walton will find the best of trout fishing in the neighboring streams, ponds, and lakes, and declare with Isaak, that angling "has a calmness of spirit, and a world of other blessings attending upon it," as he spends the long days of summer in his favorite sport.

Rutland is distant from Troy 83 miles; Albany 93; New York 234; Bellows Falls 53; Boston 167; Whitehall, N. Y. 25; Saratoga Springs 63; Lake George 60 miles. On the north is Burlington, 67 miles, and farther still Montreal, 167 miles. Fares are as follows: from Burlington, $2.00; Montreal, $4.50; Troy, $2.50; Albany, $2.60; New York, by Railroad, $5.50; by Steamboat, $3.50; Whitehall, $0.75; Saratoga, $2.24; Bellows Falls, $1.60; Boston, $4.60.

On leaving Rutland, should the tourist prefer to ride across the country by carriage, sending his baggage by rail, he can easily procure horses, and proceed to White River Junction, through a most delightful region of country. A daily stage also runs between Rutland, Woodstock and White River. The distance is nearly 40 miles, and can be travelled in a day, if one chooses, though the attractions of the way might well cause him to linger on the route. The road passes through the pleasant villages of Mendon, North Sherburne and Sherburne, around the base of Mt. Killington, and through the Green Mountain range, at this point descends along the Queechee River, through Bridgewater into Woodstock. This quiet and charming town is the county seat of Windsor County, and contains a celebrated Medical College and an Arsenal belonging to the United States. It has a population of little more than 3000. Departing from Woodstock, the road winds along, by the Queechee, leaving, at a short distance on the right,

QUEECHEE VILLAGE, which instantly recalls Miss Warner's pleasant book, of the same name, and perhaps written among these scenes, and soon reaches its termination at WHITE RIVER village in the town of HARTFORD.

Should the choice fall upon travelling by rail, the tourist will find the pleasantest scenery all along the Rutland Railroad. The stations are at some distance from the villages, whose inhabitants the road accommodates, with but one or two instances. CLARENDON is a mile or more from the central part of the town, which has a celebrated medicinal spring. CUTTINGSVILLE is in the north-eastern part of WALLINGFORD. At MOUNT HOLLY, the traveller will notice the deep cut through the solid rock, extending a considerable distance. This is the summit of the road, as it crosses the mountains. LUDLOW lies pleasantly on a little stream, a branch of Black River, several hundred feet below the Railroad, and presents a cheerful appearance, as one looks down upon it from the lofty position of the track. It is a manufacturing and agricultural town of some importance, containing about 2000 inhabitants, and has a bright, thrifty aspect. PROCTOR'S and DUTTON'S are in CAVENDISH, a pleasant town. GASSETTS' accommodates the small village of BALTIMORE; BARTON'S the town of SPRINGFIELD; CHESTER, and ROCKINGHAM, the towns of the same name, and the trains arrive at BELLOWS FALLS, in 2½ hours from RUTLAND.

BELLOWS FALLS, by this route, is distant from New York 287 miles. Fares by this route from New York, by rail, $7.00; by boat to Albany, $5.00.

From this point he continues up the Valley of the Connecticut to White River, and thence by Littleton to Franconia as on the 114th and following pages.

Distances to Franconia are as follows: From Boston by way of Fitchburg, Keene, and Bellows Falls, 224 miles; by way of Lowell and Concord over the Northern Railroad 214 miles; by way of Concord over the Boston, Concord and Montreal

Railroad to Wells River, 195 miles; to Plymouth, thence by stage, 148 miles; from New York by way of Troy and Rutland, 400 miles; by way of Hartford, Springfield, and Bellows Falls, 345 miles. Fares from Boston, either route, $7.00, by stage, $6.25; from New York by boat to Albany, rail to Rutland, &c., $9.50; by rail to Albany, &c., $11.50; by way of Hartford, &c., $10.50. Time from Boston, by Littleton, 13 hours, by Plymouth and stage 10. Time from New York, including stoppages at Rutland and Bellows Falls, 37 hours.

We have completed the description of the routes to the mountains as well as the description of the mountains themselves. We have seen that all the various routes are condensed, in reality, to three, as we approach the mountain region; one leaves us at Gorham, on the eastern side; the second at White Mountain Notch; and the third at Franconia. Whichever one may be chosen, we would urge that the whole range, from Franconia to the "Glen," be visited if possible. In no other way can a complete idea of all the beauty and loveliness of this "Switzerland of America" be gained. It is well, also, to go by one, and return by another route. Tickets *to* and *through* the region should not be purchased at a distance, as circumstances may render it desirable to vary from a plan first laid down. Travellers coming from the Canadas, either by Burlington, or by the Grand Trunk Railway, should especially avoid purchasing through tickets with privilege of visiting the mountains on their journey. To use these tickets, travellers are compelled to leave the mountains at the place where they first approached, and must thus, frequently, needlessly retrace their steps.

WILLARD'S HOTEL.

This House is so located as to offer superior inducements to the Travelling Public, as a

"Shady Retreat from the Heat of Summer!"

Connected with this Establishment is a LIVERY STABLE, and Fishing and other parties visiting the

LAKE AND VICINITY,

WILL BE FURNISHED WITH THE BEST OF

HORSES AND CARRIAGES AND EQUIPMENTS.

Bowling Alleys, Swings, &c., attached to the House.

A. L. MORRISON, Landlord.

GILFORD, (Laconia Station.)

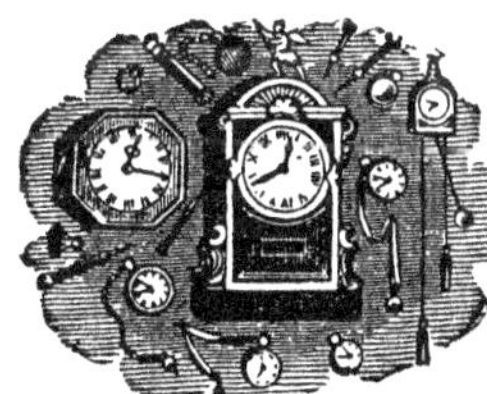

WATCHES & JEWELRY!

Whitford & Drew

SUCCESSORS TO CARTER & WHITFORD,

DEALERS IN

Watches, Clocks, Rich Jewelry, Silver Ware,

AND FANCY GOODS.

PERSONAL ATTENTION will be given to **Watch Repairing,** and all work will be warranted to give *perfect satisfaction.*

☞ All kinds of Jewelry repaired in the best manner. We have a large stock of Rich Jewelry, and feel confident that we can suit all customers, with High or Low Priced Goods. We have a good assortment of **FANS** constantly on hand, together with all the goods usually kept in a Jewelry Store. Also, Agents for **Grover & Baker's** Celebrated

FAMILY SEWING MACHINES,

NO. 184, MAIN ST., EAGLE HOTEL BLOCK;

Concord, N. H. **WHITFORD & DREW.**

Concord, Manchester & Lawrence
RAILROAD.

Passenger Trains will run as follows :

Leave Boston, from the Boston & Maine, or Boston & Lowell Depots, at 7:30, A. M., 12:00, M., and 5:00, P. M.

Leave Lowell or Lawrence, at 8:30, A. M., 1:00 and 6:00, P. M.

Leave Nashua, at 9:05, A. M., 1:35, and 6:35, P. M.

Leave Manchester, at 9:45, A. M., 2:00, and 7:00, P. M.,

Connecting at Concord with trains of the Boston, Concord and Montreal, and Northern and Passumpsic Railroads, making the shortest, quickest and pleasantest route to the

WHITE AND FRANCONIA MOUNTAINS.

No Change of Cars or Baggage between Concord & Littleton.

Trains leave Concord for Boston, Lowell, Lawrence, &c., at 5:30 and 10:15, A. M., and 4:00, P. M., or on the arrival of trains from the above named roads, making close connection at Nashua with trains of the Worcester & Nashua Railroad, for New York, Springfield, and the West. The 4:00, P. M. train is Expressed through to Norwich, connecting with Steamers COMMONWEALTH and CONNECTICUT for New York.

J. A. GILMORE, Supt.

Concord, May 25, 1858.

www.ingramcontent.com/pod-product-compliance
Lightning Source LLC
LaVergne TN
LVHW021400110826
845150LV00007B/1726

* 9 7 8 1 4 2 5 5 1 3 1 4 6 *